I have seen (as far as it can

be seen) many persons changed

in a moment from the spirit of

horror, fear, and despair to

the spirit of hope, joy, peace.

John Wesley

HOPE

An Advent Journey

OLU BROWN

Market
Square
BOOKS

HOPE

An Advent Journey

©2020 Olu Brown, dba Culverhouse LLC

books@marketsquarebooks.com
P.O. Box 23664 Knoxville, Tennessee 37933

ISBN: 978-1-950899-15-9
Library of Congress: 2020943132

Printed and Bound in the United States of America
Cover Illustration & Book Design ©2020 Market Square Publishing, LLC

Publisher: Kevin Slimp
Editor: Kristin Lighter
Post-Process Editor: Ken Rochelle

Scripture quotations taken from the COMMON ENGLISH BIBLE unless noted otherwise:

Table of Contents

CHAPTER ONE
A Reason for Hope

Throughout the Christian calendar, Advent is one of the most exciting and joyous times of the year as we await the birth of Jesus Christ. His birth is a reminder of God's love for all of humanity, and through God's grace, we have been given a wonderful gift. Out of all of the gifts we receive in life, the most significant and precious is the gift of Jesus and the salvation He offers through His sacrifice on the Cross of Calvary. This gift of salvation is forever, so we rejoice with the angels who announced His birth, and we give God praise and glory for all that God has done in our lives.

Advent is a season of reflection and rejoicing. "The word 'Advent' is derived from the Latin word *adventus,* meaning 'coming,' which is a translation of the Greek word *parousia*...the season of Advent lasts for four Sundays leading up to Christmas."[1] During Advent, worship communities place a wreath (in the sanctuary or auditorium) with four candles in a circle that are placed in the center of the wreath. Each candle represents a particular Sunday of Advent.

---

1   Justin Holcomb. (2014, November 23). "What is Advent?" Christianity.com. https://www.christianity.com/christian-life/christmas/what-is-advent.html.

- The first Sunday of Advent is the purple Prophecy Candle, which symbolizes hope.

- The second Sunday of Advent is the purple Bethlehem Candle, which symbolizes faith.

- The third Sunday of Advent is the pink (or rose) Shepherd's Candle, which symbolizes joy.

- The fourth Sunday of Advent is the purple Angel's Candle, which symbolizes peace.

- The fifth candle, a white Christ Candle placed in the middle of the wreath, may be set aglow on Christmas Eve and symbolizes the life of our Savior.

During the Advent Sundays and celebrations, there are songs, sermons, prayers and praise, all announcing the birth of the coming Savior and celebrating the season. Some songs that you may hear during Advent are, "I Want to Be Ready;" "O Come, O Come, Emmanuel" and "Soon and Very Soon."

Some of the scriptures that may be read are:

> *Israel, wait for the Lord – from now until forever from now!*
> **Psalm 131:3**

> *Comfort, comfort my people! says your God. Speak compassionately to Jerusalem, and proclaim to her that her compulsory service has ended, that her penalty has been paid, that she has received from the Lord's hand double for all her sins!*
> **Isaiah 40:1-2**

He says, I listened to you at the right time, and I helped you on the day of salvation. Look, now is the right time! Look, now is the day of salvation!

2 Corinthians 6:2

A model prayer that you may hear during Advent is:

Merciful God, you sent your messengers the prophets to preach repentance and prepare the way for our salvation. Give us grace to heed their warnings and forsake our sins, that we may greet with joy the coming of Jesus Christ, our Redeemer, who lives and reigns with you and the Holy Spirit, one God, now and forever. Amen."[2]

In addition to prayers, there are several liturgical rituals which mark the season that churches can celebrate, such as wearing clergy stoles matching the colors of the season, varying paraments on the altar and liturgical decorations throughout the church. Some examples of these, found in *The United Methodist Book of Worship,* may be, "...a Chrismon tree (an evergreen tree covered with white monograms of Christ) and a Jesse tree (a tree with signs of the ancestors of Christ). Other symbols include trumpets for Isaiah, messianic rose star of Jacob, and fleuer-de-lis."[3]

As you can see, Advent can be a very special ceremonial experience for those who follow the historic traditions of the Church: a time when family and friends gather in their local faith communities, reflect on the year and give God thanks for the coming of the new year. Some churches

---

2 *The United Methodist Book of Worship.* "Advent" (Nashville: The United Methodist Publishing House, 1992), 245.

3 Ibid., 238.

3

allow groups of individuals to serve as liturgists on each of the Advent Sundays and take turns reading the liturgy to allow the expression of the people and their voices to go forward in worship. It is a very enriching experience and a time for people to connect to one another and their Creator. It also is a time when traditions, rituals and sacred expressions of the season may not be fully expressed, and congregations recognize the season in their own contextual way. There are no set rules or traditions that you have to follow other than knowing that the season is not about you and what you desire, but about Jesus and who He was and is to the world.

2020: A Year of Unexpected

Embark on the Advent journey with an open heart and mind and with a sense of gratitude. 2020 has been a year that no one expected, and as churches planned 2020, some of them said that this year would be a year of vision. I serve as one of the pastors of a church in metro Atlanta, Impact United Methodist Church, and each year, we get very excited about the upcoming year and do our best to plan ahead. Although we didn't adopt the theme "2020: A Year of Vision," we still believed God had something great in store for the year.

As churches planned for 2020, no one could have believed that just a few months into the New Year, the entire world would shift through the Coronavirus (COVID-19), experience worldwide protests against police brutality, nor that people would encounter other life altering events such as the loss of careers and family members.

Now that we are at the end of 2020, we can say it has been a journey. Not only was 2020 a year of vision, it was also a year of sickness, protests, loss and lamenting. As the year progressed, Advent came early for me because I chose not to wait until the end of the year to expect Christ. I claimed Christ each second, minute, hour, day, week and month of 2020 and refused to write the year off as a loss and I truly expected 2020 to be the best year yet. Call me a hopeless dreamer but I believe in a power that is greater than sickness, pain and despair. It is the power of our Savior, and Advent is the time when we have to reclaim this power if we have lost it along the way and see ourselves in a different way.

> **We must see ourselves receiving the greatest gift of all, the gift of Christ.**

Christ, the Greatest Gift of All

We must see ourselves receiving the greatest gift of all, the gift of Christ. This magnificent gift isn't only once a year during Advent: it is now. Jesus is with us now, and because of His presence, we can sing the words of a great hymn, "...because He lives, I can face tomorrow."[4] This hymn, "Because He Lives," is an appropriate song to sing during Advent, but more so to believe during Advent, because it is about Jesus being born into the world and giving us hope for a new day and new way of living.

---

4   Bill and Gloria Gaither. Lyrics to "Because He Lives." https://www.lyrics.com/lyric/26588550/Bill+Gaither/Because+He+Lives. Accessed July 12, 2020.

There are so many people who are not looking forward to tomorrow, next week or next year. Life has placed them in an awful space and it is difficult to see beyond where they are right now. Part of the hope of Advent is embracing the future even when it is uncertain. On this Advent journey you will be challenged in many ways. And one of the most consistent challenges you will receive is to embrace the future and to live life in a way that shows the world that you know Jesus lives. He died and was crucified and through His resurrection, we live and live more abundantly. The first verse of the song explains the essence of Advent:

> How sweet to hold a newborn baby
> And feel the pride and the joy that he gives
> Oh but greater still, the calm assurance
> We can face uncertain days because He lives.[5]

This Advent, we await the newborn baby, and we also celebrate that He is already here. Take the journey through this book and trust that God will meet you at every page and chapter. Discover what it means for Jesus to be Heaven on Earth and how through Jesus we have an opportunity for forgiveness and grace, and to receive new life.

Emmanuel: God is With Us

On this journey, you will be reminded that God is with us (Emmanuel) and that He promised to never leave us and to be with us always. You will light the Christ Candle

---

5 Ibid.

and reclaim (and claim) the presence of Christ in your life and the world. As you take this journey, know you are not alone, and although the world may be tossing and turning and may be more chaotic than you can handle, hold on, life and living will get better.

Jesus is our reason for hope, and we know that whatever state our lives may be in at the moment, we can live, and we can have hope. Hope is the outcome of Advent and we can never postpone our hope, especially in times like these. The journey you are taking will lead you to the hope that you may have lost along the way and will help you share the hope that you rediscover with those you love. Thank you for taking the journey of Advent.

CHAPTER TWO
Heaven on Earth

Candle: Prophecy Candle (Purple) / 1st Sunday of Advent

Symbol: Hope

Scripture: Isaiah 9:6

> *For to us a child is born, to us a son is given;*
> *and the government shall be upon his shoulder,*
> *and his name shall be called Wonderful*
> *Counselor, Mighty God, Everlasting Father,*
> *Prince of Peace.*
>
> **NIV**

Prayer:

> *Dear God, as we light the Prophecy candle and are*
> *grateful for Jesus, give us knowledge to understand*
> *what you have spoken through the ages by your*
> *prophets and strength and hope to wait until it comes*
> *to pass. Amen.*

On any given day, you may hear the word Heaven mentioned in a casual conversation or referenced on a television show or on social media. Heaven is that mystical and spiritual place that people believe their loved ones reside who are no longer living, and where they hope to go when their lives on Earth are complete. During Advent, the word "Heaven" is more than a high frequency use word, it is an exceptional word, and we are called to see and know that Jesus' presence on Earth represented Heaven on Earth, and that our lives can never be the same again. Each day we experience Heaven as we welcome Jesus into our lives and reflect on the prophecy of Isaiah 9:6 that has sustained generations and created a sense of hope as they looked to the future of the fulfillment of the prophetic word. This hope was the guarantee of a future event that would impact their lives through the birth of a Savior and King.

An Eschatological Hope

It is what theologians call *eschatology:* "Study of the last things or the end of the world."[6] Sounds a little doom and gloom, but not when you join the word with hope, and it becomes eschatological hope. This refers to faith in the future that God's promises will come to pass. This is not doom and gloom, but hope and joy for the future.

The powerful image filled words in Isaiah 9:6 are some of the most inspiring and vivid words in the Bible. This prophetic announcement to people who had waited for the coming of a king whose very birth would change their circumstances was a breath of fresh air, although none of them would be living when the prophecy was fulfilled.

---

6   Donald Kim. *Westminster Dictionary of Theological Terms* (Louisville, KY: Westminster John Knox Press, 1996), 92.

This is the essence of statements such as, "You are the answered prayer of your ancestors." As in biblical times, our modern-day ancestors taught us what those during Isaiah's era felt as they waited on the prophecy to come to pass. Both our immigrant and slave ancestors understood that waiting and believing – through an eschatological hope – would always end in joy.

Later in Isaiah Chapter 40:31, it speaks of waiting:

> *...those who wait for the Lord shall renew their strength, they shall mount up with wings like eagles, they shall run and not be weary, they shall walk and not faint.*
>
> **NSRV**

The art and discipline of waiting is not easy, especially when a community of believers has been waiting for hundreds of years. Very few people want to wait and very few people are really good at waiting. When I was a child, I quickly realized that I had no special gift or talent when it came to patience and waiting. Isaiah 40 was not my goal because I always wanted everything right away. To be honest, now that I am an adult I still feel the same way and struggle with patience and waiting.

As a child, I wanted school to end for the summer break. I wanted Christmas gifts under the tree before Christmas, and Thanksgiving dinner to be ready quickly and hear the adults say, "It's time to eat!" Waiting is a skill and an ability to know that someday the wait will be over and the time it takes to receive the blessing or promise on the other side of the waiting is worth it. That is the essence of eschatological hope: to be able to live in a moment, even if it is a moment of despair, knowing that one day life and living will be better. This type of eschatological hope is seen throughout the prophetic books in the Bible.

Prophetic Books of the Bible

In the Protestant Bible, there are a total of 17 prophetic Old Testament books divided into two categories: *Major* and *Minor Prophets*.

The Major Prophets are:

- Isaiah
- Jeremiah
- Lamentations
- Ezekiel
- Daniel

The Minor Prophets are:

- Hosea
- Joel
- Amos
- Obadiah
- Jonah
- Micah
- Nahum

- Habakkuk
- Zephaniah
- Haggai
- Zechariah
- Malachi

The difference between a Major and Minor Prophet is not the content or importance of their books, rather the length of the book. Essentially, word count.

Isaiah was a major prophet with more than 60 chapters that spoke both hope and despair to the people of Israel living in the post-exilic era. Isaiah begins with hope for reconciliation to God the Creator and ends with God's judgment and God's grace and mercy ready and available to forgive.

The prophetic books in general are viewed as key historical texts, genres of both doom and gloom as well as hope and salvation. Prophecy and the prophetic books speak of the future and what is to come. Prophecy also mandates that the receiver remain present in their current situation until the prophecy is fulfilled. This limbo living is like juggling several balls in the air while trying to respond to a text message that you haven't received.

Isaiah had a prophetic word for a people who were experiencing exile and whose hopes and dreams had been dashed by their current circumstances. Prophecy may bring hope, but the hope is sometimes spoken in the midst of hopeless situations. Isaiah's words lived and flowed throughout the Jewish community for hundreds of years. Then suddenly the promise and the wait met in time and, unto us a child named Jesus was born, who was Heaven on Earth and good news for all of humanity.

And so, what does Isaiah 9:6 have to do with Heaven? Everything! Jesus being on Earth was the actual incarnation of God Almighty existing among humankind. In the Christian tradition, we celebrate the Trinity: God, Christ and the Holy Spirit.

We believe each is individual and identical at the same time. Therefore, the presence of Jesus and the Holy Spirit is also the presence of God. Theologically, Jesus' birth on Earth is the same as God being present with humanity and it doesn't get any better than that.

What About Heaven?

Let's explore it a little more. For many years, I have been a fan of Mitch Albom, and his wonderful works of fiction and his fascination with the afterlife. Recently, I read *The Next Person You Will Meet in Heaven,* which is a follow up to *The Five People You Will Meet in Heaven.* Both books talk a lot about Heaven and life after death. As you read these novels, it is so easy to transition from Earth to Heaven and be caught up in a new and different world above.

Like Mitch, I, and so many others, have been puzzled with the afterlife and what happens when we take our last breath on Earth and travel to the next destination. As Christians, we are firm believers in Heaven and believe that Heaven is this wonderful place that the Bible speaks of with many descriptions and illustrations.

One of the most well-known descriptions is from John's gospel which describes Heaven as a place with many mansions (John 14:2). The mansions in Heaven are much grander than the mansions on Earth. Picture a sprawling estate with beautiful gardens and golden walkways leading up to the most magnificent home you have ever seen in your life. The windows are as clear and bright as a beautiful sunny day. The entry door to the mansion is made of pure gold with wonderfully carved flowers along the surface. The furniture is designed by angels and similar to pieces you would see in a luxury furniture gallery. Beyond the interior layout of the home, there is a peace and calmness that is beyond imagination and comprehension: a peace and calmness that reassures you that you are finally home.

Another description the Bible gives is Heaven having many magnificent gates leading into the city and the streets are paved with gold (Revelation 21:21). Each of these is a trustworthy description of Heaven and creates a panoramic picture in the human psyche of what Heaven really looks like and how it is designed. Heaven from the Bible's viewpoint is a wonderful and glorious place where there is the richness of joy and overflowing peace.

Even though the Bible gives vivid and clear descriptions of Heaven, in most cases, people are introduced to Heaven long before they read scriptures in the Bible or hear a sermon about Heaven. Descriptions of Heaven live out loud in our culture, and unconsciously, we receive these images. They build slowly but surely in our mental databases and develop and shape our view of Heaven.

When someone dies, the words may be uttered by a family member, "They are in Heaven, a better place."

When someone tastes a delicious dessert, and the flavor is still on the tip of their tongue, they may exclaim, "Wow, this tastes like Heaven."

When you have traveled and stayed in a hotel, during check-in you expected the economy room you booked online but were informed by the hotel that you will be staying in the best room on the property, and when you opened the door to the room you exclaimed, "This is Heaven."

When people describe Heaven, it isn't always from the Bible, but from culture and from those persons who have described and interpreted Heaven for them along the way. We take the stories of Heaven and the images that have been shared, and we design Heaven for ourselves.

In Hebrew, the word Heaven, *marom,* is also used (Ps. 68:18; 93:4; 102:19) as equivalent to *shamayim,* "high places".[7] Whenever someone describes Heaven, their description is typically upward to this place beyond the stars, at the top of the universe where God, Christ, angels and those who have died reside.

We see this upward glance towards Heaven in the Book

---

7   M.G. Easton. *Easton's Bible Dictionary* (New York: Thomas Nelson, 1897).

of Acts, Chapter 1, during Jesus' ascension. When Jesus was lifted up, the angels standing with the disciples asked:

> *...why are you standing here, looking toward Heaven? This Jesus, who was taken up from you into Heaven, will come in the same way that you saw him go into Heaven.*
>
> **Acts 1:11**

When Jesus returned to Heaven, in a single moment the focus of the disciples' gaze shifted upward. Not only did the disciples believe the GPS coordinates to Heaven were in the sky, but as we talk about heaven 2,000 years later, we still have a tendency to look up.

As a pastor, I have had the honor of spending time with people during their last days and moments on earth. I often wondered, when they closed their eyes for the last time on Earth and opened them in Heaven, "What did they see?"

- Did they see clouds, blue skies and an impressive mansion in the distance where their bodies were transfigured, and they became angels with wings and glorious voices?

- Did they see those who had died before them and instantly reconnect, just like old times?

- Did they see Jesus and experience the absolute presence of God and their voices lifted in praise and worship and shouted like Isaiah, "Holy, holy, holy is the Lord of Heavenly forces! All the Earth is filled with God's Glory!" (Isaiah 6:3).

A Christian music group named Mercy Me introduced a song in 1999 entitled "I Can Only Imagine" that almost twenty years later in 2018, became a movie bearing the same name as the song. This song raised questions about life after death and the endless possibilities of Heaven. Mercy Me envisioned what Heaven would look and feel like only to conclude that at best we are left to our imaginations when it comes to Heaven. The opening verse of the song says:

> *I can only imagine what it will be like*
> *When I walk by Your side*
> *I can only imagine what my eyes will see*
> *When Your face is before me*
> *I can only imagine...*[8]

When we think about Heaven, we are left imagining what Heaven will truly be like and we are fortunate to have beautiful songs and words that comfort until the day we discover Heaven for ourselves. For hundreds of years, the Israelites imagined what the fulfillment of the prophecy in Isaiah 9:6 would look like and never perceived that when the prophecy was fulfilled, they would experience Heaven on Earth. Although the Israelites could not fully articulate the future experience of the prophecy coming to pass, I believe they thought their world would never be the same once the prophecy took place.

That is the power of prophecy in that it shifts our world and our experiences when it comes to pass. We have

---

8   Mercy Me. Lyrics to "I Can Only Imagine." https://www.azlyrics.com/lyrics/mercyme/icanonlyimagine.html. Accessed July 16, 2020.

this deep and abiding feeling that the fulfillment of the prophecy will happen in God's time and when it happens, life will be on another level.

The day Isaiah 9:6 spoke of would be a day when Heaven was a little closer to Earth, and the angels would rejoice by singing "Hosanna in the highest." Isaiah 9:6 was the foretelling of Jesus coming to Earth as a human living among humanity. It is important to note that Jesus' birth symbolized a new era for the Israelites and His birth was connected to the lineage of King David.

Consider the connection to Jesus and David in Matthew's gospel:

> *So there were fourteen generations from Abraham to David, fourteen generations from David to the exile to Babylon, and fourteen generations from the exile to Babylon to the Christ.*
> **Matthew 1:17**

The people hoped and dreamed of a ruler who would lead and guide them into the future with justice and virtue. It would not have been out of the ordinary for the Hebrew people to hope that the "child" spoken of in Isaiah would be similar to King David. Not only was Jesus in the family line of David but to the people waiting for the prophecy to come to pass, David was the archetype for the future king.

The latter part of Isaiah 9 describes the child as having "authority," and whose name will be "Wonderful Counselor, Mighty God, Eternal Father, Prince of Peace." Those were some big expectations placed on Jesus long before He was born on Earth, and when He arrived, no one could have imagined that a king would be born in a manger outside with animals.

The Birth of Jesus

The symbolism of His lowly birth speaks volumes to our world today. It is unfortunate that too often we may discount or discredit someone because of where their position or stage begins in life. Even though we know that all people are created in the image of God, and we are called to love and respect each and every person, discounting them without getting to know them is always an easier short-term ploy. In the long run, however, we miss out on getting to know some of the most gifted people in the world.

It is unfortunate that too often we may discount someone because of their position or stage in life.

I believe even today some might be slightly disappointed that Jesus did not come as a warrior, but rather as a humble healer for a sick humanity. Jesus was not David, and that was a blessing because Jesus chose to come in a form in which all of humanity could relate.

Isaiah's description of Jesus in Chapter 9 can leave believers in a lurch when they compare Isaiah's prophecy to the life of Jesus in the Gospel accounts in the New Testament. The opportunity we have is to see Jesus for who He was and is, and not what we want or wish Him to be.

Not only is it important to think about the symbolism of His humble birth, it is also vital to consider the actual date of His birth, December 25, which holds great significance and speculation as well. There has been a lot of conversation about Jesus' birthday and whether or not it was on December 25 or another day in the calendar year.

Valerie Strauss, a reporter for *The Washington Post* summarized the Christmas birth debate in a 2015 article entitled, "Why is Christmas on Dec. 25? A brief history lesson that may surprise you."

She offered the following reflection:

> *Dec. 25 is not the date mentioned in the Bible as the day of Jesus's birth; the Bible is actually silent on the day or the time of year when Mary was said to have given birth to him in Bethlehem. The earliest Christians did not celebrate his birth. As a result, there are a number of different accounts as to how and when Dec. 25 became known as Jesus's birthday.*[9]

I know for those of you reading this reflection for the first time, it may be shocking, and Christmas will never be the same. Let me caution you that although you may give up on Christmas after reading the quote from the article, don't give up on Christ.

As an adult reflecting on my childhood years celebrating

---

9 V. Strauss. (2015, December 15). Why is Christmas on Dec. 25? A brief history lesson that may surprise you. *The Washington Post.* https://www.washingtonpost.com/news/ answer-sheet/wp/2015/12/25/why-is-christmas-on-dec-25-a-brief-history-lesson-that- may-surprise-you/.

Christmas, I sometimes cringe at how caught up I was on the commercial side of Christmas and not the spiritual side of Christ.

Although I never debated whether or not the date of Jesus' birth was December 25 or put emphasis on it, I acted as if Christmas was my birthday; instead of focusing on the Savior, I focused on the number of toys and gifts I would receive.

Mike Slaughter's words in his book, *Christmas Is Not Your Birthday,* hit me like a ton of bricks during my time of reflection on Christmas as a child. Mike said:

> *Sometimes we worship tradition more than we worship Jesus, preferring the comfort of the familiar to the challenge and risk of doing something new. Honoring Jesus this Christmas may require the creation of some new traditions that are more focused on what Jesus wants from us than on what we desire ourselves.*[10]

Like many, I have found myself caught up in the commercialism of Christmas and forgot to focus on the real meaning of Christmas – which was, and is – Jesus. Mike was right: whether Jesus birthday was on December 25 or another day, it wasn't my birthday, it is Jesus' birthday. More importantly than focusing on the day Jesus was born and using it as an opportunity to buy all of the gifts for ourselves and others that we can, it is vital this Advent that we focus on the fact that Jesus was born,

---

10 Mike Slaughter. *Christmas Is Not Your Birthday.* (Nashville: Abingdon, 2011), 67.

and this is a tremendous blessing for the world. Don't get fixated on a day and the commercialism of Christmas. When we really think about Jesus' birth, the date of His birthday is not more important than His life.

Beyond the date Jesus was born, His birth in general was extraordinary because He was conceived by the Holy Spirit. Even Mary couldn't quite make it work in her mind. For example, when she questioned the Angel Gabriel who informed her of her future pregnancy, Gabriel answered:

> *The Holy Spirit will come over you and the power of the Most High will overshadow you. Therefore, the one who is to be born will be holy. He will be called God's Son.*
>
> **Luke 1:35**

Theologically, this is spectacular. Even though Jesus was born into a sinful world, He wasn't a sinner because He was conceived by the Holy Spirit. Isn't that awesome! Because He was sinless, He was the perfect sacrifice for all of the sins of humanity. Think about it. All of the sacrifices and rituals that were required in the Old Testament could all be one sacrifice through Jesus. Amazingly as a sinless being, He still understood the sins and temptations of the world.

In Luke 4, right after Jesus' baptism and God saying, "You are my Son, whom I dearly love; in you I find happiness" (Luke 3:22), Jesus immediately went into the wilderness, and for 40 days was tempted by the devil while fasting from food.

Jesus' ability to experience temptations was the intersection of humanity and divinity. His humanity experienced tests and trials and through the power of His divinity and God's Word, He was able to overcome every temptation.

The Power of Advent

We must never forget that Jesus felt and experienced temptation while on Earth. The power of Advent in part is the realization that Jesus was both human and divine and that we have a Savior who can identify with the pain and suffering of our world and our human experiences. Therefore, when you pray this Advent, consider beginning with the phrase from Isaiah 9:6. Here is an example:

> *Dear God, for unto us a child is born, and I thank you that He was born for me and the entire world. As an adult, He felt pain, suffering and temptation. Give me strength and faith to endure life as my Savior endured even unto the cross. Like Jesus, I know even in persecution, crucifixion and death, I will be victorious.*

You are free to add your own words and phrases to this model prayer but don't forget as you pray, Jesus has experienced what you are experiencing.

In addition to Jesus understanding our human experience, His birth, through the lens of Heaven on Earth, also represented hope for our world. As we fight a global pandemic, injustice, hunger and poverty there is hope in Jesus. His birth made a global impact of hope and healing 2,000 years ago and still makes an impact today.

What was the hope Jesus brought to Earth? What was the blessing?

Isaiah says it later:

> *...by his wounds we are healed.*
>
> **Isaiah 53:5**

The hope and blessing are that we are ultimately healed from pain. Healed from despair. Healed from heartache. Even healed from a pandemic that has altered and changed the entire global landscape. We can celebrate Jesus' birth not only because was He born for us, but He also died for our sins and everything we would face on Earth. This global impact created an everlasting connection between Heaven and Earth that can never be reversed or erased. That is hope.

The fact that Jesus was Heaven on Earth as the incarnation of God Almighty should not be a surprise. Since creation, God has always been connected to Earth. From the biblical point of view, in Genesis, God is the creator of all things including humanity, who lived first in the Garden of Eden. Beginning in Genesis and ending in Revelation, God is consistently connected to humanity.

Even in times when people disobeyed, God's grace and mercy was present and willing to forgive. God's most impactful connection to humanity was when Heaven touched Earth by presenting a child who was the Savior of the world. And today, the one who was a baby born in a manger is our Savior, who died on the cross and leaves us the comfort of the Holy Spirit that constantly reminds us of God's presence and power.

Through Jesus' birth, there was a renewed connection that emphasized God as Creator and Jesus as Savior of the world. During human tragedy and turmoil, such as a pandemic or natural disaster, it helps to maintain a deeper connection with the Creator to know that God has not forgotten about us and our situations. In a recent conversation with a wise young person, he reminded me that we have to stay connected to God in tough times. Not only do we have to stay connected during tough times, but also during the good times. It's the strength and support we receive during the good times that sustains us when times are not going so well. It is similar to building up a reservoir of goodness that will be used later when life and living seem upside down.

Reflecting on Difficult Times

In my own life, when I sit and reflect over the most difficult times I have experienced when life felt upside down – if I am honest with myself – God has always been present and has never left me. I have always experienced the closeness of Heaven.

Over the past summer, I had a goal of placing all of my sermons and speeches from previous years on a digital cloud file. I came across three sermons from 2010. Eulogies, to be specific. In 2010, I preached the eulogies of three people who impacted my life in tremendous ways.

Our church was only a few years old. Looking back, this was a trying season for me professionally due to having to navigate overcoming sorrow and loss on a big scale.

The first eulogy was in April of 2010 for a woman named Sandra Webb Walker. I met Sandra in 1999, when I arrived in Atlanta the summer after finishing undergrad at Jarvis Christian College. I came to Atlanta to begin seminary at the Interdenominational Theological Center and to work as a youth pastor at Cascade United Methodist Church. Cascade blessed me and two of my buddies by allowing us to live in the church's parsonage. Although we were grateful, we quickly realized there was no furniture in the house, and we had to hustle. One day, while I was at work learning the ins and outs of being a youth pastor, little did I know that Sandra had recently become a widow, was a retired educator, and had decided to share her time and talents with Cascade serving as a receptionist for the church.

While I was in the office, she overheard me mention my need for furniture, and she said out loud, "I have a couch."

Of course, I was surprised and overjoyed, but I remembered I had a Honda Civic and it was not designed to transport couches.

Astonishingly, she must have heard what I was thinking and the next words out of her mouth were, "I have a truck." Sandra and I didn't know it, but that introductory conversation would be the beginning of a friendship that helped me during my early days in Atlanta and connected me to a person who was like a mother to me.

A little more than 10 years later, Sandra passed, and I had the privilege of preaching her eulogy. My opening words recalled our first conversation in the office at Cascade: "I have a couch, and I have a truck."

The second eulogy was for another dear friend, Bill Bradley. Bill's funeral was in June, a couple of months after Sandra's. I met Bill after our church started in 2007, and I can't remember the specific year or month when Bill and I connected, but it was a mutual blessing.

Bill had a former career in finance and accepted his call to ministry later in life. He went to Drew Seminary and returned to Atlanta where we later met. Bill was a sharp dresser, astute in theology, witty and wasn't afraid to tell me or anybody the truth. Bill connected with Impact during the time when we were looking to purchase our initial property and move out of the public school. His wisdom and support will always be appreciated.

I remember while attending one of our Saturday morning team meetings with Bill, he didn't look so well, and shortly thereafter was hospitalized. I went to the hospital to pray with him before his exploratory surgery and neither one of us realized it would be the last time we would talk.

During our last conversation, his energy was waning and you could tell he wasn't in the best of health. We talked about the dreams and plans for the new church building and how it would be renovated.

Bill looked at me and said, "Make it pretty." Bill never recovered from surgery and passed away shortly thereafter. I will never forget Bill and the wisdom he gave me. Bill would always say, "It is what it is."

The third eulogy was for a young man, Bobby Tillman, who was 18 years old. Bobby and his family lived in a suburb near Atlanta and attended Impact Church. One Saturday night, Bobby and his friends went to a party and, sadly, four young men decided to jump him, ultimately beating him to death. The news was absolutely horrific and a shock to the city, state and the nation.

I remember sitting in the courtroom during the trial for one of the young men who killed Bobby and hearing the judge tell the young man that he was sentenced to life in prison and feeling my heart drop. When I reflect on the sadness of Bobby's death and those who took his life, I often think we lost five young men on that tragic evening. One to death, and four to the criminal justice system. Since Bobby's death, his mother, sister and family have carried on his legacy, and I know Bobby is in Heaven looking down on them with a smile.

During Bobby's eulogy, I tried to encourage the family with these words, "Bobby transitioned on Sunday and Jesus got up on Sunday...He's okay."

Bobby Tillman passed in November 2010 and will never be forgotten. His legacy will always live on.

Now, more than 10 years after each of these persons have passed, we still miss them and the only thing that has helped us move forward is our connection to Christ.

It is true, through Christ we have Heaven on Earth, and it makes it a little easier knowing one day we will see them again in the Heaven above.

Like you, I don't have any special claim or secret steps to get through hard times, but I do know that, with Christ, we can make it. I have had more difficult years since 2010 and I'm sure I will have more, but my hope is in Christ – not in the minute, hour, day or month. It is not the moment that determines the outcome, but the One who is in the moment with us. That is Christ.

Feeling Heaven All Around You

There are times and moments when Heaven feels a little closer to Earth and you no longer have to gaze upward to see Heaven, but you can feel Heaven all around you.

There is a famous story about a boy flying a kite that rises into the clouds, and a man passes by and asked the boy a question: "How do you know the kite is still there if you can't see it?" The boy replied with a smile, "Every once in a while, I can feel a little tug."

Heaven on Earth is that moment when you can feel a tug on your lifeline that gives you strength and encouragement to hold on a little while longer.

- It is the tug of encouragement that a grandmother feels who is raising five of her grandchildren on a limited income.

- It is the tug of hope for a cancer patient when their medical team informs them that their body is responding to the new treatment.

- It is the tug of praise for the high school student when she receives an email stating she has been accepted into the college of her dreams.

- It is the tug of comfort for the person who buried their loved one and realized they will never see them again on this side of glory.

These are Heaven tugs that are necessary in hard times and helps see us through to the next stage that allows us to hold on.

As we reflect on the reality of Heaven being closer to Earth through Christ, we also have to acknowledge that Heaven, though joyous, brings about feelings of grief and loss.

Easter 2020

Our worship planning team sketched Easter 2020 nearly a year earlier with team members, large pieces of paper on the walls, refreshments on the table, and excitement in the air. We were so proud that for the first time in a long time, we were ahead and planning Easter well before the actual day. We never thought our world would be in a pandemic and Easter experiences would be watched primarily from living rooms and kitchens via smart phones, laptops and televisions.

No one could have ever predicted Easter 2020 would be 100% online. In addition to the worship platform of Easter being different, we also would not have imagined that on Easter weekend, tornadoes would rip across the southeastern part of the United States of America leaving homes destroyed and people displaced claiming more than 30 lives.

With the numbers of deaths from a global pandemic and horrific weather, there has been a lot of conversation about grief and loss and how virtually everyone in the world has been touched by grief and loss. Loss is inevitable in life, but loss becomes more difficult when it is unexpected and unplanned.

Our church receives many notifications about families experiencing grief and loss, and in some cases when the loss was expected the news isn't as jarring, but in other cases when it is unexpected, the news rocks us to the core.

In these times we are called to comfort grieving families in their time of loss and remind them that "God knows" their pain and suffering. God sent Jesus because God knew humanity was hurting and heartbroken. And the same way God knows our pain, God also knew and understood the pain Jesus experienced.

God knew Jesus was suffering in the Garden of Gethsemane when Jesus said:

> *My Father, if it's not possible that this cup be taken away unless I drink it, then let it be what you want...*
>
> **Matthew 26:42**

God knew the pain when Jesus took His last breath on the cross and uttered:

> *Father, into your hands I entrust my life. After He said this, He breathed for the last time.*
>
> **Luke 23:46**

God Knows

In each of the moments of grief and loss in our lives, the comfort of Heaven seems to come a little closer when we understand "God knows." Whenever we are deep in life's challenges and we have every reason to give up and throw in the towel, it can be difficult to see the sunshine and know that better days are ahead.

As you are reading this book today and you are celebrating Advent, I know it is not easy and you may be tempted to surrender to the difficulties of life, but I encourage you to hold on a little while longer and trust that God really knows and cares about what you are experiencing and going through.

You are not going through life alone and even in the most challenging times, life is worth living. Because God knows, there is hope. The hope I am referring to is an eternal idea and emotion that gives us protection and courage in periods of chaos and despair. The great theologian Henri Nouwen would argue that prayer and hope are intertwined, and we have seen over the years how people in the midst of trying times have discovered hope through prayer. Nouwen wrote, "In the silence of prayer you can spread out your hands to embrace nature, God and your fellow human beings. This acceptance means not only that you are ready to look at your own limitations, but that you expect the coming of something new. For this reason, every prayer is an expression of hope."[11]

---

11 Henri Nouwen. *With Open Hands,* (Notre Dame, IN: Ave Maria Press, 1972), 63.

Wow! Nouwen said what I wish I could say to myself and others when we are struggling. "Every prayer is an expression of hope."

During and after Advent, keep praying and know that whether you pray short, long, eloquent, scripted, extemporaneous, or childlike prayers, they create hope. Your prayers matter to God, and even when you don't feel like your prayers go higher than the ceiling in the room where you are praying, keep praying and believing.

Each word you utter is a sound of hope that is heard by God and hope will never disappoint you. Romans 5: 4-5 says this about hope:

> *...endurance produces character, and character produces hope. This hope doesn't put us to shame, because the love of God has been poured out in our hearts through the Holy Spirit, who has been given to us.*

Therefore, don't be ashamed of your life or struggle. Each day you are getting stronger and God is giving you hope. Today is a new day! Keep praying. Keep believing. Like Nouwen, you will find the reassurance of hope in prayer. Hope has a way of infiltrating your pain and despair and reassuring you that all will be well.

As you are reading this section, I can hear you asking, "I understand hope, but what about faith?" There are times when hope and faith are used interchangeably, but the two are uniquely different and equally important.

Faith is believing in someone or something. The Bible

declares faith as, "...the reality of what we hope for, the proof of what we don't see" (Hebrews 11:1).

Faith allows one to have a deep and long-lasting belief that an event will take place, or a promise will be realized. When a parent tells a child that they will take them on a vacation to a wonderful theme park next summer, the child has faith or belief in the parent, and therefore, they look forward to summer vacation.

Faith is necessary to exist in life and navigate our ups and downs so that we eventually arrive at a place where our belief outweighs our anxiety and fear. Hope is more about assurance. Remember the song, "Blessed Assurance"?

> *Blessed assurance, Jesus is mine,*
> *oh what a foretaste of glory divine.*

Through hope we have assurance of the outcome and in spite of the processes we may endure, we choose through hope to hold fast to the promise.

Jesus being Heaven on Earth gives us hope and faith each day such that we are able to live with joy because we know that God knows, and we know that Jesus is with us. This Advent Season, as you read Isaiah 9:6 out loud and light the purple candle of prophecy, don't say the liturgy as if it were from some distant place and time.

Although Isaiah was written thousands of years ago, the prophetic words "For Unto Us..." are a current and real truth that Jesus never left us and is still with us. Say the words as you read them with power, authority and gratitude for a prophecy fulfilled.

I hope you aren't disappointed like those who grew up reading Isaiah and were there when Jesus was born and noted that He didn't look, fight or act like King David or another warrior in their era. They almost missed Heaven and Jesus because Heaven and Jesus never look like we think they should. This Advent, open your eyes and your heart so you can see Heaven and Jesus. When you can see Heaven and Jesus, you are no longer waiting on Advent to take place, you are living Advent because you will fully be aware of Jesus' presence and grace in your life.

Questions for Reflection:

1. When you imagine Heaven, what are some of the words and phrases you use to capture the picture in your imagination?

2. Is Heaven an actual place or is it being in the presence of God? Explain.

3. Have you ever waited on God's promise to come to pass in your life? How long did it take? What did you feel when it happened?

4. Write your own advent prayers for each week. What are some of the words and phrases you would use? Who and what would you pray for? What are you grateful for?

5. This Advent season, what does Jesus' birth mean to you?

CHAPTER THREE
Opportunity for Forgiveness and Grace

Candle: Bethlehem Candle (Purple) / 2nd Sunday of Advent

Symbol: Faith

Scriptures:

Micah 5:2:

> *As for you, Bethlehem of Ephrathah, though you are the least significant of Judah's forces, one who is to be a ruler in Israel on my behalf will come out from you. His origin is from remote times, from ancient days.*
>
> **NIV**

Isaiah 61:1-2:

> *The Spirit of the Lord God is upon me, because the Lord has anointed me to bring good news to the afflicted; He has sent me to bind up the brokenhearted, to proclaim liberty to captives and freedom to prisoners; To proclaim the favorable year of the Lord and the day of vengeance of our God.*
>
> **NASB**

Prayer:

> *Dear God, help me to have faith in Jesus Christ and*
> *to believe like a child without pretense or reserva-*
> *tion. I thank you for choosing Bethlehem to be Jesus'*
> *place of birth and you have shown me that even those*
> *places and things that may seem like the least of*
> *these are important and special to you. Thank you*
> *for using my life and the lives of others to impact the*
> *world. Amen.*

Do you remember singing the Christmas hymn, "O
Little Town of Bethlehem," written by Phillips Brooks? It
was noted that Brooks, "...wrote this beloved Christmas
hymn for the Sunday School children at his Philadelphia
parish, Holy Trinity Church, following a pilgrimage to
Bethlehem in 1865."[12]

The following is the first verse of the hymn:

> *O little town of Bethlehem,*
> *how still we see thee lie;*
> *above thy deep and dreamless sleep*
> *the silent stars go by.*
> *Yet in thy dark streets shineth*
> *the everlasting light;*
> *the hopes and fears of all the years*
> *are met in thee tonight.*[13]

The little town of Bethlehem would be recorded in

---

12 Hawn, C. *History of Hymns:* "O Little Town of Bethlehem" Discipleship Ministries. https://
www.umcdiscipleship.org/resources/history-of-hymns-o-little-town-of-bethlehem.
Accessed July 14, 2020.

13 Ibid.

history as the birthplace of Jesus and will always be remembered and celebrated. The prophet Micah described Bethlehem as:

> *...though you are the least significant of Judah's forces, one who is to be a ruler in Israel on my behalf will come out from you.*
> **Micah 5:2**

It is like the quintessential small beginnings or underdog story that you hear of a well-known scholar, athlete, entertainer, humanitarian or business leader who was born in a small town and becomes a superstar. If you have ever heard of one of those stories or biographies, you may know about the little town of Bethlehem. Most people are first introduced to Bethlehem through the Gospels of Matthew and Luke.

About Bethlehem, Matthew wrote:

> *After Jesus was born in Bethlehem in the territory of Judea during the rule of King Herod, magi came from the east to Jerusalem.*
> **Matthew 2:1**

Luke wrote:

> *Since Joseph belonged to David's house and family line, he went up from the city of Nazareth in Galilee to David's city, called Bethlehem, in Judea.*
> **Luke 2:4**

Obviously, there has to be more to the city than a place you pass that has a big billboard flashing, "The Birthplace of the Savior of the World."

The Birthplace of Jesus

This isn't to say that Bethlehem – the birthplace of Jesus – isn't significant, but like every great underdog story, there are always more details and history to be discovered. The connection to Bethlehem as "David's city" in Luke 2 is a detail that must be explored and offers a hint of some of its history.

In the Old Testament, Bethlehem is mentioned often and literally means, "The House of Bread." Rachel, the wife of Jacob, died and was buried in Bethlehem after giving birth to Benjamin. A significant part of the story of Ruth is based in Bethlehem, and Bethlehem is the home of King David's great-grandfather Boaz. King David was also born in Bethlehem.

In population and notoriety, Bethlehem may not have been high on the Google search engine at the time of Jesus' birth. Yet it had a proud and rich history of leadership and influence. It was in Bethlehem that Jesus was born outside in a manger because there was no room in the hotel. The Savior of the world was born in the cool night air next to barn animals and was wrapped in cloth to keep His body warm.

Luke provides a descriptive verse about the birth. "She gave birth to her firstborn child, a son, wrapped him snugly, and laid him in a manger, because there was no place for them in the guestroom" (Luke 2:7).

We know Mary and Joseph had other children because the text mentions Jesus was their firstborn child. We also know that the hotel where they were staying had no vacancies, and He was born outside, which was a metaphor of His life. Jesus birth, primary ministry and even death were all outside. If the hotel manager knew what the world knows now, the manager would have found a way for Jesus to be born on the inside of the hotel. Maybe the manager would have quickly added an additional room by brokering a deal with one of the modern-day reality home renovation show hosts who literally renovate an entire home in less than one hour (with at least three commercial breaks).

Although it was not convenient for Mary and Joseph nor was it the best environment to have a newborn baby, I am glad Jesus was born on the outside, and not the inside of the hotel. Sociologically, it signifies Jesus being connected to the marginalized and outsiders even from the moment of His introduction into the Earth. His birth was Heaven on Earth, and it was not the scene you would have expected for the one that Micah and Isaiah spoke of in their prophetic books.

One commentary describes the scene of Jesus' birthplace:

> *At Bethlehem, we also witness the scandal of the Christmas story. Neither the familiarity nor the season's festivities should prevent us from realizing the scandal that God came into human history completely helpless, as a newborn, and was laid in a feeding trough...God was born on the road. The crib was a feed trough, and those who came to visit were shepherds, not kings.*
>
> *By entering human history in this way, God identified with the powerless, the oppressed, the poor, and the homeless."*[14]

---

14 R. Culpepper. *The New Interpreter's Bible, Vol IX.* "The Gospel of Luke" (Nashville: Abingdon Press, 1995), 66-67.

The birth of Jesus at Bethlehem was a statement to the world that God is present and for humanity. This was a radical statement and counter-cultural in nature.

In Chapter 2, I mentioned Heaven doesn't always look like Heaven, and consequently, we can miss it. Micah 5:2 concludes:

His origin is from remote times, from ancient days.

There was no indication that His beginning on Earth would start outside, next to livestock. There must have been great concern and disappointment experienced by those who read Micah and Isaiah and held out hope for a warrior king and Savior who was born into pomp and circumstance: the type of king everyone celebrates and trends on social media.

From the very beginning of Jesus' life, He was counter-cultural and seemed to be the exact opposite of what people expected, but He was the very thing they needed. Perhaps His parents even questioned or had their doubts. Remember, an angel visited both Joseph and Mary and informed them of what was to come. But, the angel skipped the minor details that their son's birth would be in a manger and shortly after His birth, they would need to develop a nomadic mindset given that His life and purpose would be threatened.

They thought for a moment as they were looking at their new life in a manger with their newborn baby, "We didn't sign up for this."

Luke begins with Jesus being born outside and ends with Jesus dying outside on a cross between two thieves.

But thanks be to God, they hung in there and persevered to the very end: the result was salvation for the world.

This is why people like movies and stories about underdogs. We can always cheer for them even when we don't think they stand a chance. Because of the circumstances of Jesus' birth, the environment around Him, and the threat against His purpose, He was in an underdog category.

This is seen in the outsider motif in Jesus' birth narrative in Luke's gospel. Luke begins with Jesus being born outside and ends with Jesus dying outside on a cross between two thieves. Part of the symbolism of Jesus' life in Luke's Gospel is that Jesus was never an insider and was always an outsider. He wasn't born with pomp and circumstance on the inside of a beautiful hotel or hospital. All of these facts combine to illustrate the life of a Savior who gives hope to those who could never find their way to the inside or to those who were never allowed on the inside: the underdogs of society.

The outsider motif is a reality that the great poet Langston Hughes illustrates in his post-Civil War, Jim Crow era poem, "I, Too."

> I, too, sing America.
> I am the darker brother.
> They send me to eat in the kitchen
> When company comes,
> But I laugh,

And eat well,
And grow strong.
Tomorrow,
I'll be at the table
When company comes,
Nobody'll dare
Say to me,
"Eat in the kitchen,"
Then.
Besides,
They'll see how beautiful I am
And be ashamed—
I, too, am America.[15]

Hughes's poem is a social critique even today, "They'll see how beautiful I am." These words reveal a deep desire to be wanted, accepted and approved by those who society says matter.

Hughes is referring to racial inequality, which we still see today, among the other forms of inequality (such as sexism and ageism). Like Langston Hughes' poem, many people question their beauty and wonder if others will fully accept them as they are. Hughes' powerfully speaks for the second-class citizens, those excluded from mainstream culture. The poem portrays African Americans being forced outside and not able to eat inside at the table. The character in the poem dreams of the day for full equality, full recognition of beauty under the law and to eat at the table when company comes.

We would hope that almost 100 years after Hughes penned, "I, Too," the world would be different and that all

---

15 Arna Bontemps. *American Negro Poetry.* (New York: Hill and Wang, 1964), 64.

of God's children are viewed and treated as the beautiful beings that they are, but this is not the case.

The battle for equality and justice continues for citizens of America as they demand that the eloquent words of the Declaration of Independence would be more than words and hold true for all people:

> We hold these truths to be self-evident, that all men are created equal, that they are endowed by their Creator with certain unalienable Rights, that among these are Life, Liberty and the pursuit of Happiness.[16]

Little did we know that the words of this great document were written for insiders and not outsiders. Even today, so many people struggle and hope to one day sit at the table and be fully welcomed and accepted. I believe this is why so many people who have been historically oppressed have found hope in Jesus, because He too was oppressed and marginalized by those in power that He came to save.

Jesus is the Hope for All People

Throughout the ages, Jesus has always been the source of strength for those who have been denied justice and equality. For those in need of grace and mercy. For those who weren't born into the right circumstances or family. Jesus has always been the hope of equality for those who have been marginalized and oppressed and never

---

16 National Archives. (n.d.). *Declaration of Independence: A Transcription.* https://www. archives.gov/founding-docs/declaration-transcript. Accessed July 16, 2020.

invited, or welcomed, to the tables of government, enter-
prise, education, civic groups or upward mobility. For
immigrants pressing to find their way in a new land.
For enslaved Africans forced into hundreds of years of
slavery and Jim Crow in the land of the free and home of
the brave. For those in modern-day slavery forced into
the abysmal bondage of human trafficking and their
bodies being used and abused for the pleasure and wealth
building of others.

Jesus is the hope for all people, nations and the world
in need of forgiveness and grace. Being born outside is
never a good circumstance, but for Jesus, it was necessary and the blessing that helped complete our salvation.
Listed in the section on Jesus' birth certificate for "Place
of Birth," the word 'outside' is printed. Jesus was an
outsider, an underdog.

Through the years, I have had the opportunity to talk
with a lot of people, and there are times when our conversation takes place during a crisis in their lives. A consistent
comment I hear is, "No one understands what I am going
through." Their words are absolutely true in that as an
individual having a unique experience, there is no one in
the world who can fully understand what they are going
through. Without offering a challenge to their statement but
a perspective of hope, I reply, "No human on Earth understands what you're going through, but Jesus understands."

Today, this is true for each and every one of us, and
our hope is in knowing that Jesus knows and Jesus cares.

Isaiah reminded us:

> *He was pierced because of our rebellions and crushed because of our crimes. He bore the punishment that made us whole; by his wounds we are healed.*
>
> **Isaiah 53:5**

It is hard to convince someone in crisis that Jesus knows and cares, but it is true. Jesus really understands and knows what we are going through and experiencing. Henri Nouwen comes to our aid once again through his book, *The Wounded Healer,* where he so eloquently helped us to see Jesus as a wounded healer and through His woundedness healed the world. He wrote, "But this is exactly the announcement of the wounded healer: 'The master is coming—not tomorrow, but today, not next year, but this year, not after all our misery is passed, but in the middle of it, not in another place but right here, where we are standing.'"[17]

That is the word of hope for people who are suffering. It tells us that Jesus is not on the way, but Jesus is right here walking with us through our pain and suffering.

Over the summer, something happened at our church that was a vivid and current reminder of hope that is only found in Jesus as our wounded healer. During a virtual staff meeting after the weekend when another black man was killed by a police officer, the meeting started with a

---

17 Henri Nouwen. *The Wounded Healer* (New York: Image Doubleday, 1972), 102.

soul check-in to gauge where the team was emotionally. The death of the person took place just a few miles from our church campus.

There were feelings of anger, hurt, pain and confusion during the soul check-in moment with our staff, and thankfully, the space was safe for team members to share their hearts, fears and concerns. While the moment was very difficult, a feeling of hope broke through in the space that was tangible and not superficial.

The hope was not a quick or temporary hope that left us with a spiritual high where we would be okay in the moment and then return to sadness after our spiritual high ended. Nor was it a superficial hope that simply covered our pain with cliché phrases that many believers say in times of despair like, "It will be ok, keep your head up, and stay encouraged."

Rather, it was a hope grounded in the story of Jesus born on the outside in a small town called Bethlehem, who never seemed to be politically correct or willing to conform enough to make it to the inside. Our hope was found in Jesus who was born and died on the outside. The hope of Jesus our wounded healer who understood the pain and the hurt felt by our team. It is the mark of a wounded healer when he or she is able to have emphathy for those who are hurting and relate to their suffering.

As we concluded our staff meeting, somehow and someway we knew that we would make it through with the ever-present hope of Jesus Christ. Not only would we make it, but our city, nation and world would make it because as believers in Christ, we hold out hope for all the world. It is the same hope that Jesus shared with the world. Jesus never kept hope to Himself or His inner circle but shared it along His ministry journey.

- He gave hope to John the Baptist and reassured him that his ministry was not in vain.

- He gave hope to the sick as He healed them and restored their faith.

- He gave hope to His disciples by teaching them to fish for people.

- He gave hope to a woman at a well who became the first woman evangelist in the New Testament.

- He gave hope on the cross as He welcomed a criminal into paradise.

Perhaps this is the hope that Jürgen Moltmann spoke of in his book *Theology of Hope,* "Hope is nothing else than the expectation of those things which faith has believed to have been truly promised by God."[18]

Moltmann understood hope and what it meant to find and discover hope even as a prisoner of war. The hope he described had implications for the Church of Jesus Christ:

---

18 Jurgen Moltmann. *Theology of Hope* (New York: Harper and Row Publisher, 1967), 27.

This hope makes the Christian Church a constant disturbance in human society, seeking as the latter does to stabilize itself into a 'continuing city.' It makes the Church the source of continual new impulses towards the realization of righteousness, freedom and humanity here in the light of the promised future that is to come.[19]

Through a global pandemic, protests in the streets and with great theologians like Nouwen and Moltmann, our role as Christians and leaders of the Church of Jesus Christ is reaffirmed. We are called to show and uphold a different kind of hope that is eternal and unwavering. This hope can only be found in Jesus, who was born off the beaten path in Bethlehem and grew up to be the Savior of the world.

With the testimony of Jesus' wounds and His hope, we have an opportunity to celebrate Advent and to embody Advent in everything we are and do. We are the Church of Jesus Christ and if there is any institution or organization that should always have hope, it should be the Church. How we serve and share the love of Christ is always through a modality of hope and inspires others to see the world in a different and positive way.

Hope Impacts Worship

As the Church, this hope also impacts the way we worship. Before COVID-19, most worshipers were deeply committed to worshiping and connecting with God, Christ and the Holy Spirit within the four walls of their faith communities.

---

19 Ibid, 22.

The same was true for our church and many of those who worshipped with us. Church was no longer wherever God was, but where we chose to meet God within our buildings. We were guilty of limiting God to our four walls. When COVID-19 caused our in-person worship experiences to cease, and churches shifted to virtual worship only, I was blown away and never thought anything like this could happen.

Although the tag line of our church is:

Doing Church Differently™

and we always took great joy in being a progressive and technologically savvy church, this new normal of 100% virtual worship was a major adjustment.

After getting over my pity party and embracing the new normal, I quickly learned that our church had invested and emphasized in many good things over the years to communicate the gospel and reach people for Christ. But in a single week, we were back to the basics.

I learned that God could not be contained within our buildings, and although people were disappointed that we weren't meeting in our building, we had to show them and remind them that God was bigger than our buildings. That church didn't start and end in an hour or more, but that church was any and everywhere. We had to remind worshippers that Jesus was born on the outsde and our traditions and limited faith had restricted Jesus to the inside of the walls we made called church buildings and that moving forward we had to hold fast to Jesus' lesson on worship, "God is spirit, and it is necessary to worship God in spirit and truth" (John 4:24 CEB).

In addition to being convicted to worship outside of the walls in "Spirit and Truth," I also learned that when people got over not being in the building, what they wanted the most was authenticity from leaders, preachers and teachers. COVID-19 caused many to have anxiety and fear and they looked to places like the Church for encouragement and support, and became instant experts in discerning what was real versus what wasn't. Authenticity was the highest priority of the day and where and how worship took place shifted to a lower priority.

I was mesmerized as people discovered and rediscovered, they could actually worship God from a live stream while at home. There were people who did something even more radical which was to shop around on other church websites and watch worship experiences they never considered watching before. Shockingly, many of them enjoyed the experiences and discovered the same way God moves at their church, God also moves at other churches and denominations. Pastors and worship leaders who were normally leading worship in front of people on stages suddenly realized that leading worship and preaching in their kitchens, living rooms or empty church buildings was possible and that God's Word and Spirit could be translated through live recordings on websites or pre-recorded experiences posted on social media. I saw people living out the genuine "Spirit and Truth" of worship for the first time.

People were able to strip away the pomp and circumstance of worship and solely focus on the true essence of worshipping God and deeply connecting with their Savior. For many people, experiencing a global pandemic, the disruption of their everyday lives, and protests for freedom and justice, caused them to discover and rediscover Jesus. It is my prayer that during Advent you don't lose your focus and return to the commercial side of the season and find yourself caught up in conversations and events that don't honor God or the sacrifice of Jesus. I pray you find Jesus and focus more on Him than the despair and pain of the world we live in.

When we find Jesus, we will see His wounds and most importantly, our hope in the present and future will be renewed even if the world is different and normal isn't normal anymore. We will be able to stand and move forward because our hope is not in the world but in Jesus Christ. We will be people of hope and lead churches of hope.

One of the most tangible forms of hope found in Jesus is forgiveness and grace. If you are like me, with all that I have seen of wrong and injustice in the world, I have also seen wrong and injustice within myself, so I am personally in constant need of forgiveness and grace. This doesn't mean that I fail to hold others accountable for their negative actions, but I realize that I, too, am a sinner in need of forgiveness and saved by grace.

This Advent, I hope you place Bethlehem in your navigation app on your smartphone and find your way to God's forgiveness and grace through Jesus Christ.

What is this forgiveness and grace? It is in Isaiah 61 and repeated by Jesus again in Luke 4. You may miss it if you are reading the text as an insider and not an outsider like Christ. The language in the text is the cry, pain and protest of an outsider:

> *The Lord God's spirit is upon me, because the Lord has anointed me. He has sent me to bring good news to the poor, to bind up the brokenhearted, to proclaim release for captives, and liberation for prisoners, to proclaim the year of the Lord's favor.*
>
> **Isaiah 61:1-2a**

This is the language of forgiveness and grace, and the joy of Advent. To be healed is to have known affliction. To be whole is to have been brokenhearted. To be free is to understand the isolation of prison. To be forgiven individually and collectively is to have known sin. Just like Christ, we are called to be wounded healers and show others the way to God's forgiveness and grace.

During the time of Holy Communion/The Lord's Supper at church, as congregants ready their hearts, minds and souls, they may recite the prayer of

"Confession and Pardon."

It centers us around forgiveness and grace because as we reflect on Jesus' sacrifice for our lives, we are reminded that we are sinners saved by grace. As we approach the Lord's Table, we are aware of the frailty of our human nature and that we are constantly in need of God's grace. This prayer is not only a prayer to be prayed during Holy Communion / The Lord's Supper, but it is a prayer to speak each day of our lives as we remain focused on the ultimate sacrifice on the Cross of Calvary.

> *Merciful God,*
> *We confess that we have not loved you with our*
> *whole heart.*
> *We have failed to be an obedient church.*
> *We have not done your will,*
> > *we have broken your law,*
> > *we have rebelled against your love,*
> > *we have not loved our neighbors,*
> > *and we have not heard the cry of the needy.*
> *Forgive us, we pray.*
> *Free us for joyful obedience,*
> *Through Jesus Christ our Lord. Amen.*[20]

This prayer is more than beautiful words. It is a plea and cry before Almighty God acknowledging sin and asking God for forgiveness and grace. There are people today who are living in bondage and held hostage to the evil and mayhem in the world and who daily seek to be free. There is the false belief that freedom is external first and not internal.

One could easily think, "If only I could get a new job, make more money, be in a relationship with someone who understands me, I would be whole and happy." This is a fantasy and is as fleeting as the wind because having the things wished for in the comments above does not necessarily

---

20 *The United Methodist Book of Worship.* "Service of Word and Table I" (Nashville: The United Methodist Publishing House, 1992), 35.

create wholeness and happiness because these are mostly external. Although valid and important, they are not as important as internal needs.

Forgiveness: An Essential Need

What are some of the essential internal needs? Faith, hope, love and most importantly, receiving forgiveness and forgiving others. Forgiveness of self and others isn't easy because it involves introspection and being honest with your history and the history of others.

It seems easier to move on with our lives and to forget without forgiving, but this is not recommended for a healthy life and future. We are truly never free, nor can we move forward without forgiveness.

This Advent, go back to Bethlehem and discover forgiveness for yourself and forgiveness for others. Jesus reminded us that He was anointed to release us from the hurt and pain of today and yesterday, but we have to allow Him to release us. Receive forgiveness for yourself, forgive others and you will be free.

Not only is Bethlehem an opportunity for forgiveness, it is also the realization of God's grace. Isaiah 61 talks about the "favorable year of the Lord" and grace is God's favor, which is compassion and love.

Some have described grace as, "unmerited favor." Remember Bethlehem means, "House of Bread." I love the prayer Jesus taught His disciples in Matthew's gospel. In Chapter 6:11 it references bread, "Give us the bread we need for today." The word grace could easily be used in place of the word bread in the prayer and read as follows, "Give us the grace we need today."

Daily Grace

I have often wondered why the prayer asks for bread for today and not for every day. If it were my original prayer, I would ask for bread forever and not just one day. Considering that request with more maturity and wisdom, I now understand that if God gave me bread forever, I would begin to take bread for granted because it would be stockpiled, and each day I would likely become less thankful for the abundance of bread.

It is only when we have bread for the day that we have to trust God for bread for the next day and we are grateful for every piece because we know is present for only a day. With this daily gratitude, my prayer would be:

> God, thank you for my daily bread that you don't have to supply or give. I am grateful for your care and generosity towards me.

Interchanging the word, "grace," I would also pray:

> God, thank you for my daily grace that you don't have to supply or give. I am grateful for your care and generosity towards me.

When we use the word "grace" in place of "bread," we are telling God, "Thank you for the grace that you have given me today." Theologically, I understand and believe that God's grace for us is in abundance and lasts more than one day.

God's grace lasts for a lifetime, but what if we gave God thanks for "Daily Grace" and although grace is in an abundance, we don't allow a single day to end without telling God, "Thank You for grace."

As you light the purple Bethlehem candle this Advent, thank God for a little town called Bethlehem where an outsider was born. Thank God for forgiveness and the ability to forgive others. Thank God for bread and grace for today.

Questions for Reflection:

1. Like Jesus, have you ever felt like or been treated like an outsider? What was the experience and how did it make you feel?

2. Is there a time when you forgave yourself or someone else and it created a new wholeness within? How did it feel? Was it difficult to arrive at this moment in your life?

3. What does hope look like to you and how do you know when you have it?

4. What is your definition and example of grace? Have you ever taken grace for granted?

5. Have you ever underestimated someone because of their circumstance, family of origin or economic status? Did you discover you were wrong in passing judgment on them? How did this change the way you saw them as person?

CHAPTER FOUR
Possibility for
New Life in Christ

Candle: Shepherd's Candle (Pink or Rose) / 3rd Sunday of Advent

Symbol: Joy

Scripture: Luke 2: 8-11:

> [8]*Nearby shepherds were living in the fields, guarding their sheep at night.* [9]*The Lord's angel stood before them, the Lord's glory shone around them, and they were terrified.* [10]*The angel said, "Don't be afraid! Look! I bring good news to you—wonderful, joyous news for all people.* [11]*Your savior is born today in David's city. He is Christ the Lord.*

Prayer:

> *Dear God, help me to be open and present to your glory and all that you want to announce in my life. At times I feel unworthy and wonder why you choose me but I am grateful, and I surrender to your call and favor for my life. Let me be filled with joy as I look to the future and overcome the fear of what you have in store for me. Amen.*

The announcement of Jesus' birth happened with an angel telling a group of shepherds:

> *Don't be afraid! Look! I bring good news to you—wonderful, joyous news for all people. Your savior is born today in David's city. He is Christ the Lord.*

> **Luke 2:10-11**

My elementary school English teacher would have been pleased and excited with the two brief sentences in verses 10 and 11 that are filled with adjectives, adverbs, verbs and even an exclamation mark. This would have been a model sentence to diagram and explore the various syntax structures in the English language. Though Luke was not an English teacher, he concisely penned these two sentences to chronicle the most famous birth narrative in history, the birth of Jesus. It was penned so well that children around the world participate in Christmas plays and perform dressed as angels, blaring out the birth announcement of Jesus Christ, sometimes so loudly that the audience has to cover their ears and hold back the joyful laughter caused by seeing little children having fun.

These two verses painted a high definition image of what the shepherds saw and felt in the middle of a field off the grid and under a dark evening sky illuminated by stars light years away. The only competition to the starry constellation was an angel identified as the "Lord's Angel," who suddenly appeared illuminated by the glory of the Lord.

At first sight, the shepherds wondered if one of the stars had fallen from the sky, but this could not be, because stars don't talk. This was not a fallen star. This was an angel in their very presence. The two concise verses are broken into four revealing phrases:

- Don't be afraid! Look! (Affirmation)
- I bring good news to you—wonderful, joyous news for all people. (Confirmation)
- Your Savior is born today in David's city. (Salvation)
- He is Christ the Lord. (Continuity)

Don't be afraid! Look! (Affirmation). Before the good news could be revealed, the angel had to do some pre-work to first affirm the shepherds and encourage them to not be afraid and to continue looking. This would seem odd at first, but the context in which the angel appeared was not ordinary, and as a matter of fact, it was absolutely extraordinary. Contemplate going about your daily routine and suddenly seeing an angel before you. Not only is the angel in your presence, but the angel is also talking to you.

I don't know anyone who doesn't like angels, but for most, this would still be a little unnerving and amazing at the same time. It's like one of those moments when you say to yourself, "Is this really happening?" When the angel appeared, fear immediately set in. There are instances in the Bible when angels appeared to people to give good news, and instead of the recipients rejoicing and being excited, they were afraid and raised questions.

For example, when God called one of the Judges of Israel named Gideon through an angel, Gideon's response was:

> *With all due respect, my Lord, if the Lord is with us, why has all this happened to us?*
>
> **Judges 6:13**

Have you ever had a "With all due respect" moment with God? This typically happens when God asks you to uproot your life and move to a different state and city to seek out a new job you haven't even applied for.

You tell God, "With all due respect, I am comfortable in my current home, city and job. Please find someone else."

What about Zachariah, who was John the Baptist's father? When he received the news (through an angel) that he and his wife, Elizabeth, would have a child, the Bible clearly states:

> *He was startled and overcome with fear.*
>
> **Luke 1:12**

His verbal response to the angel was:

> *How can I be sure of this? My wife and I are very old?*
>
> **Luke 1:18**

This is one of those "Is someone spamming my email" moments that we experience from time to time. It is the email with the subject line that reads, "Click and Win $10,000!" As tempted as you may be to click and read the email, there is something within that brings pause and you hesitate to move forward. Zachariah hesitated because he was afraid, and he also felt God might have been spamming his email. Have you ever felt pranked or tricked by God, and in addition to your fear, felt embarrassed? You felt embarrassed because you weren't sure if you could share this news with anyone since you didn't know if the opportunity was real.

Life Changing News for Mary

Mary, the mother of Jesus, can also attest to how it feels when angels appear with life changing news from God. Historians believe that Mary was a teenager, and although she and Joseph were engaged, they weren't married.

These were the right ingredients for a great rumor to spread throughout her hometown of Nazareth. Can't you see the Twitter feed?

> **Teenage girl, might be pregnant by fiancé, not 100% sure. Some say the Holy Spirit is the Father.**

That story would spread like wildfire on social media. When the angel approached Mary and told her the destiny God had in store for her, the angel used similar words that were used with the shepherds:

> *Don't be afraid, Mary. God is honoring you. Look!*
>
> **Luke 1: 30-31**

Mary's response to the angel was a question of biology because she was utterly surprised. She asked the angel:

*How will this happen since I haven't had
sexual relations with a man?"*

Luke 1:34

It is safe to say that whenever angels appear sharing
the destiny God has for you, chances are, it will be bigger
than your wildest imagination and only God can make it
happen. Therefore, the chance for doubt, fear and questions are highly likely.

Walking by Faith

If you are experiencing any concern or doubt as you
await God's promise and prophecy for your life to come
to pass, you are in great company. You are friends with
Gideon, Zachariah and Mary the Mother of Jesus.

Walking by faith and trusting God is never easy
because we typically want all of the details and the fine
print of the plan before we take the first step. This is often
the opposite of faith because faith means that we may take
the first step and get the details later.

Caution! This doesn't mean you live your life haphaz-
ardly without preparation, and whenever things don't
work out you blame God. Rather, you pray, plan and
prepare and when you don't have all the details, you trust
God in the gaps and you move forward.

When God's plan is revealed for your life, you will never
have enough money, support, resources or supplies to
make it happen but it will be okay. If you had each of those
things you wouldn't need God and you wouldn't need faith.

See, faith has a way of making up the difference and the deficit. I hope God's plans for your life are always so grand that it surprises you and you ask God crazy questions. Sometimes the crazier the questions, the bigger the plan. Life without surprises is not living but simply existing.

In the midst of grand moments when God is informing us that our lives will never be the same, fear has a way of arresting us and of attempting to convince us to remain where we are physically, spiritually and mentally. It is very possible to allow fear to cause you to get stuck on the edge of your miracle.

How many regrets have been shared by those who lived long enough to look back over a panoramic video of their lives and come to a place of admitting that some of their greatest moments never happened because fear caused them to become trapped before walking towards their miracle?

Getting trapped can play out in so many different ways from careers to other life choices that we make along the way. To live is to face fear and whenever we face fear, we have to consider the source of the fear and determine if it is real or not.

In 1933, when the United States was in the middle of the Great Depression, President Franklin D. Roosevelt, in his first inaugural speech, offered these reassuring words to an anxious nation:

So, first of all, let me assert my firm belief that the only thing we have to fear is fear itself—nameless, unreasoning, unjustified terror which paralyzes needed efforts to convert retreat to advance.[21]

Living through recent economic challenges in America, we may have a better idea of how the Great Depression Era generation felt economically and emotionally. To be elected President in the middle of the Great Depression had to have been daunting. Roosevelt, as a courageous leader, talked directly to the citizens and helped them face their fears head on. Fear can be described as an emotional and mental response to difficult and unknown experiences that we face in life.

As irrational as fear might be at times, it isn't irrational to the person experiencing it because fear is contextual. What causes one person to be afraid may not cause another person to be afraid, and that is the power of contextual fear. It has the ability to infuse itself in our human experience and cause us to become trapped in our minds and our emotions. When fear sets in, it is difficult to be open to what God is saying and doing in a particular season in our lives.

I am not saying that people living during the Great Depression and other difficult times in history should not be afraid, but even in the worst circumstances, there are opportunities to manage one's fear. Though, this is easier said than done.

---

21 National Archives. (n.d.). *Inaugural Address of the President.* https://www.archives.gov/files/education/lessons/fdr-inaugural/images/address-1.gif. Accessed July 16, 2020.

My Grand Resolutions

At the close of each year as I prepare for the new year, I have a tendency to set grand resolutions, and the grandest of them all is that, "I will not be afraid next year."

This resolution normally doesn't last past the first hour of the New Year, and I am back at square one, being, thinking and acting afraid. I wish I had a better spiritual report for you, that along with my role as a pastor, I am also a superhero, but I am not. Most times, I am just a big ball of fear functioning in society like everyone else.

Because I have a tendency to give myself over to fear and anxiety, over the years, I have invested a lot of time in personal counseling with professional therapists trained to hear my concerns, fears and anxieties. I have always appreciated when the therapist didn't insist my fears weren't real, but rather provided tools and techniques to confront my fears and anxieties.

With a bit of a kick in the butt from President Franklin D. Roosevelt's, "Nothing to fear but fear itself," learning how to analyze and manage my own anxiety through therapy, as well as a hefty dose of prayer and scriptures, I am less dependent on superficial New Year's resolutions and am better able to confront and overcome my greatest fears. When I can't overcome them, I have learned to live with them and press forward anyway.

Whether you are a shepherd in a field, Gideon experiencing a call from God underneath a shade tree, Zachariah thinking someone had spammed his email, Mary the mother of Jesus with questions only an angel could answer, or a newly inaugurated President, fear is fear.

The angel recognized their fears and began with a tool and technique of affirmation, "Don't be afraid."

The angel knew the shepherds were afraid, and before the angel could move forward with the good news, the shepherd's fear had to be addressed. It is not unlike your life today as you think about the experiences that God would like to introduce into your life, yet at the current moment, the fear factor seems to be greater than your faith factor. You can see and hear God's plans for your life, but as quickly as they are written, they are washed away like sandcastles losing a battle to the rising tide along a sandy beach shore.

With all of the noise you hear right now, can you hear God's angel telling you, "Don't be afraid"? These are powerful words and even more powerful if we follow them and act on the plans that God has for our lives.

To get past your fear, you may ask yourself a series of questions:

- What if I fail?
- What if they say no?
- What if the new business doesn't work?
- What if I have to move back home with my parents?

Don't be afraid to ask yourself these questions because it is helping you to face the worst that could possibly happen. When you answer the questions, remember to add, "Don't be afraid."

Be Strong and Brave

I often wondered about how in the book of Joshua, after Moses died and Joshua took over leadership of the Israelite community, God told Joshua three times to "Be strong and brave."

The very first passages in Joshua aren't strategic plans, blueprints, or conversations about warfare. Rather the opening words of Joshua are about fear and tools and techniques to help Joshua overcome his fears as the new leader of the people of Israel. In every new or continuing venture fear has to be addressed on the front end so that the entire mission is not forfeited or self-sabotaged.

God is speaking to you today in a unique way to a unique situation that is causing you to be afraid. To everyone else it seems simple and crazy, but to you the situation might as well be a mountain blocking you and your dreams. I wish that I could tell you to think your fears away, but they will be there today, tomorrow and forever. But like the angel of God, I can say you are more powerful than you give yourself credit, and you can face each and every fear in your life. Remember, "Don't be afraid."

Sometimes the fear we face is because life brings new experiences and circumstances that we have never seen or considered before. The shepherds had never seen or experienced anything like this, and they were startled by the angelic being. I can remember many times in my life when I felt like the shepherds, and my fear eclipsed the blessing of the news that was in store for me; my fear attempted to short circuit my faith.

This often happens when I am traveling in new and uncharted territory. One of these times was during a phase in our new church when we were looking for more permanent space to worship and launch ministries. Our new church started in 2007, and after we had worshiped in a public school for several years, our leaders began searching for a permanent property to purchase. This was necessary because we literally had to set up and take down every piece of worship equipment for adults and children each Sunday.

The tasks were more than a notion. Volunteers and members of our production team started in the early morning hours before worship, and long after worship ended, they were still working to take down every item they set up earlier that morning.

It was backbreaking work for Jesus, and we felt a permanent building would give our team members time back with their families and position the church for more sustainable growth. We finally located a property that was perfect for our church. The property didn't look like much on the outside or the inside, but we could see the possibilities that God had in store for us. We made an offer of $650,000 for the property which was an old warehouse that was 76,000 square feet sitting on ten acres of land in an industrial park.

Thankfully, the bank accepted our offer and we moved forward and made the purchase. After the loan closing, I can vividly remember returning to the property and taking a walk as my heart began to drop.

I know. It sounds crazy. Remember, I struggle with fear. As soon as the ink on the deal had dried, fear began to raise crazy questions in my mind during that walk around the property. Questions like:

- Did we make a mistake?

- Did we miss an environmental issue on the property that will show up later when we begin renovation and construction?

- Can we afford to actually begin construction?

- How long will this vacant property sit until we can begin to shape it into the vision God gave us?

- Will people laugh at us because we can't afford to start construction and say, "I knew they couldn't do it."

All of these questions, and more, were swirling through my mind at a time when I should have been celebrating. I was a big ball of worry and fear. Looking back on those days and how much I lived in fear, I feel that I cheated God's miracle in that experience because instead of celebrating, I was constantly worrying about how God would make a way. Oh. I forgot to mention, we paid off the $650,000 property loan in nine months.

When the shepherds saw the angel, they should have immediately started celebrating, but they couldn't because fear had eclipsed their faith. Maybe there is a miracle on the horizon of your life right now, and instead of celebrating, you are worried about how the miracle will take place. There are millions of questions going through your mind.

If this is what you are experiencing right now, take my advice and enjoy the moment and know everything will be fine. If there is one thing I have learned, it is that some moments only come once in a lifetime. You are living your God moment right now, and I hope you don't talk yourself out of celebrating because you are worried about how God is going to sustain the miracle in your life. Make a promise to yourself today. Promise that moving forward you will celebrate every birthday, every new day, every little and big win, every sunrise and sunset, and every breath.

Enjoy Your Miracles

The definition of a miracle is "a blessing or manifestation of grace that you can't explain." Therefore, if you can't explain how it arrived, you surely can't explain or worry about how it will stay.

Enjoy it!

When I think back on the closing of our church property and how I didn't celebrate, but worried first, I realize I missed a big opportunity to give God praise for a miracle that was meant to strengthen my faith and show our team the power of God and the favor of God on our church.

I've learned through my own experiences and that of the

shepherds in the middle of nowhere, if the Gospel story is about anything, it is overwhelmingly about managing fear and faith and constantly knowing God will not lead us to places where God could not sustain us. A wise person taught me, "Where God gives vision, God always gives provision."

The angel was emphatic in telling the shepherds not to be afraid, and the next word was another tool and technique to help them manage their anxiety and fear, the word was, "Look!" (vs. 10).

An ingenious technique, because fear can restrict our sight and cause us to only look to the past and not the opportunities of our present and future. God's angels are constantly telling us to not be afraid and look. Visualize a person afraid of heights, walking over a secure expansion bridge suspended between two cliffs; they are afraid to look forward and afraid to look down. Even when the guide reassures them the bridge is safe and secure to move forward, the fear of falling and heights reveals every rational and irrational fear in their lives and produces hundreds of questions why moving forward is not in their best interest.

Questions like:

- What if the maintenance on the bridge is not current?

- What if the maintenance person was distracted during a recent repair?

- What if the maintenance person was afraid of heights and didn't fully check the bridge for safety?

- What if the tour guide doesn't like me and wants to get rid of me when I am halfway across the bridge?

- What if I look down and freeze and someone has to come rescue me?

In this bridge story, there are two primary struggles: One, a fear of heights and being suspended in mid-air on a bridge that sways in the wind. Two, looking down hundreds of feet and imagining a quick and sudden death.

Let me be clear, I am not saying that fear is bad and that you should put this book down and go climb the nearest mountain or building you see. In some cases, fear is good and protects us from danger, but in other cases, fear can trap us and prevent us from taking risks and considering the new things God has in store for us.

For the person to be successful in the bridge story, they have to manage their fear of heights by remembering that the bridge is safe and the risk of falling is unlikely. They have to block out of their mind the quick and sudden death replay reel and keep moving forward with a newly recorded reel of success. To reach their goal of getting to the other side, they have to manage their fears and continue looking forward.

This is our task today and that is to keep looking forward. While I don't believe the word "Look!" was only about vision with our physical eyes, it was also about continuing to experience the glory of God and the possibilities of what God can and also will do in our lives. This type of sight is internal sight: the sight of faith.

This is what Paul meant when he was shepherding the Church at Corinth:

We live by faith and not by sight.

2 Corinthians 5:7

Powerful words that have helped so many people live on a higher level. As you celebrate this scripture, there will be times when it is hard to follow because your faith will be challenged. You may choose to look at the things you can only see and make major life decisions via your physical sight and not your spiritual sight. I can only encourage you to look again, and this time not with your eyes but with your faith, which has the capacity to look beyond barriers, obstacles and detours.

Great things have happened in the world because people chose not to look with their physical sight but with their faith. Advent is a season that tasks us to take a second look. Although we were disappointed the first time, dare in faith to look again and know God's promises for our lives will come to pass. In one of my favorite inspirational books, *The Dream Giver* by Bruce Wilkinson, the character Ordinary broke through his comfort zone by leaving a place of familiarity to follow his dream:

> *Ordinary decided. If this fear wasn't going to leave, he would have to go forward in spite of it. Still trembling, he picked up his suitcase, turned his back on Familiar, and walked to the sign. And even though his fear kept growing, Ordinary shut his eyes and took a big step forward – right through the invisible Wall of Fear.*[22]

---

22 Bruce Wilkinson. *The Dream Giver.* (New York: Multnomah, 2003), 23.

Although Ordinary closed his eyes right before he moved forward, he was still looking – not with natural sight, but with faith. On this journey of life, your natural sight will often fail you, and you have to always look with the greater sight of faith that is within you. Keep moving out of your comfort zone until you reach your dream like Ordinary and the shepherds. What is the familiar circumstance that has you stuck in a place that is not beneficial or fulfilling, but yet you remain anyway? We all have these places and times in our lives, and if we aren't careful, our sight will fail us. There is so much in store for your future and the plans that God has for you will cause you to ask a lot of questions because the plans are greater than your imagination. Remember, the greater the question, the bigger the plan.

Looking Beneath the Surface

The art of looking is about seeing deeper and knowing that what we often see and experience on the surface is only partial, and that it is not the full and complete story. Teachers are skilled in the area of seeing beneath the surface to the genuine abilities of their students and helping their innate talents shine through. I am so grateful for all of the teachers in my life who pushed me to see below the surface and reach my fullest potential to help me achieve what I thought was impossible. These teachers will forever be my angels and the voice of God telling me, "Don't be afraid. Look!"

Perhaps while in school you had one or more of these

angel teachers as well. You can remember completing an assignment and submitting it to your favorite teacher believing it was the best work you had ever done. You patiently waited for a pleasing remark and an excellent evaluation of your work. Instead, after a day or two, your teacher emailed the following evaluation, "Your work was good, it wasn't your best, and if you try harder and study more, you can submit a completed assignment that is more reflective of your abilities."

For a moment your feelings were hurt, but you quickly realized the teacher had your best interests at heart and you accepted the challenge. The teacher was an angel in disguise who reminded you to keep looking for the uncommon and subsurface potential. This teacher, like the angel who met the shepherds, refused to allow you to miss your moment.

The shepherds almost missed their moment. Earlier, I talked about regrets and getting stuck but what about missing your moment? Everyone can look back over their lives and see that one moment they missed. At the time it didn't seem big, but later it was huge.

There are a lot of different reasons why people miss their moments and I suspect their reasons at the time were valid and worthy. What if we lived and trusted in such a way that we didn't have to look back with regret, instead refusing to settle for the surface? No longer would it be okay to engage in surface careers, surface conversations or surface living.

What if this Advent you made an agreement with God and yourself?

**No more regrets or missed
moments. No more surface living.**

Lean into every God ordained moment for your life and trust that God has everything you need and is walking with you every step of the way.

The shepherds were being pushed out of their comfort zones and usual patterns. In a sense, the angel was encouraging them to stay curious which is what Brené Brown explores in her book, *Braving the Wilderness.* She wrote:

> *Curiosity is an act of vulnerability and courage...We need to be brave enough to want to know more.*" [23]

This completely prohibits having an attitude that is willing to settle for the surface or miss any God ordained moment. Brown's encouragement to modern day shepherds is to overcome fear and become confident in existing in the unknown and avoid getting stuck in the past or present. To be curious means we are called to "...surrender to uncertainty." [24]

Are you ready for more uncertainty? You might be saying, "I already have enough uncertainty in my life, and I don't need more."

I get it and you are probably right, but if you don't want to settle for the surface and don't want to miss your moment, get ready for more uncertainty, and stay

---

23 Brené Brown. *Rising Strong* (New York: Random House, 2015), 53.

24 Ibid, 52.

curious. The shepherds were bold enough to step into their unknown, stayed curious and managed uncertainty because their faith was able to bridge the gap and sustain them. The closer you get to Christ, there will be many roads of uncertainty but if you can dare to keep looking you will eventually make it to your destination.

There can be no greater uncertainty than being in the middle of a field at night, and suddenly an angel appears with a news flash that will change the rest of your life. The angel gave such an enthusiastic introduction, "Don't be afraid! Look!" because they were inviting the shepherds into the realm of the unknown, which is uncertainty. The shepherds had to remain open for the ride of their lives.

During Advent, the Holy Spirit is encouraging us to remain open to God in new and different ways, and to know that God can meet us at any place, anytime and anywhere. For the shepherds, their place was in the middle of a field with their grazing sheep.

Today, your place may be driving on a highway, flying in an airplane, working from home or running to the grocery store to pick up a needed ingredient for the spectacular dinner you are making tonight. God has no boundaries, and we have to remain open.

God told Abraham, "Leave your land, your family, and your father's household for the land that I will show you" (Genesis 12:1). And with very little notice, Abraham had to pack up his belongings and family and trust God through the next adventure (Genesis 12:1).

In Exodus 3, Moses heard the call of God on his life from a burning bush on the backside of the desert. He had to remove his shoes because wherever God is, it is holy ground.

A prophetess and judge of Israel named Deborah fought fearlessly in battle as God called her to be a victorious leader for her people (Judges 4).

After experiencing personal and economic devastation, Ruth made a pledge to her mother-in-law Naomi, "Wherever you go, I will go; and wherever you stay, I will stay. Your people will be my people, and your God will be my God" (Ruth 1:16). Her pledge to her mother-in-law and her commitment to the unknown allowed Ruth's name to be listed in Matthew's Gospel as one who was in the lineage of Jesus Christ.

Whenever an angel shows up and tells you, "Don't be afraid!" Listen, and tell your fear to take a back seat to your faith because there is no telling where God will take you if we are willing to surrender to uncertainty.

Good News: First, for the Shepherds

After the angel gave the shepherds affirmation, the angel was able to offer confirmation. The confirmation was, "I bring good news to you – wonderful, joyous news for all people" (Luke 2:10). The angel announced "good news" to a group of lowly and outcast shepherds. Before saying the good news was for the world, the angel said the good news was first for the shepherds. This is unique because in modern day journalism, fighting for top market ratings and top position in the news market, whenever "breaking news" occurs, is expected. Breaking news is always shared with the masses first.

This angel/newscaster took a different approach with the breaking news by sharing it with shepherds first and the masses second. Sharing the news with the shepherds first demonstrates how Jesus' entire life and even His birth was counter-cultural, consistently breaking the norms and doing the very opposite of what was culturally accepted to reach the lost and marginalized.

There is also more to be said about the shepherd's profession and how it was so uncommon for the news to be shared with them first:

> Shepherding was a despised occupation at the time. Although the reference to shepherds evokes a positive, pastoral image for the modern reader and underscores Jesus' association with the line of David...in the first century, shepherds were scorned as shiftless, dishonest people who grazed their flocks on others' land. [25]

If there was a VIP listing of those who would be first in line to receive the news of Jesus' birth, the shepherds would not be on the list or considered at all. It is also important to take note of the fact that the good news of Jesus' birth was not first presented to the rich and famous

---

25 R. Culpepper. *The New Interpreter's Bible, Vol IX.* "The Gospel of Luke" (Nashville: Abingdon Press, 1995), 65.

or those from respected professions. Although these individuals would typically be on a VIP list, when it came to Jesus birth, there was no list. Only a group of shepherds in the middle of nowhere. The good news was shared first with these shepherds who were struggling and managing everyday life like the masses of society.

This was a birth announcement confirming that everyone would have access to the newborn Christ and the old customs of privilege and favor would no longer be the norm. The very nature of His birth confirmed that He is for the marginalized, outcast, broken hearted; those who are down and out in life and in need of good news.

The announcement was a game changer 2,000 years ago, and today it is still good news because Advent is a time of hope and a reminder that the gift of Jesus Christ is for all people.

After the angel told the shepherds the good news was for them personally, the angel said, "...wonderful, joyous news for all people" (Luke 2:10).

Wow!

The Purpose of Advent

The sequence of this narrative speaks directly to the purpose of Advent and Christ. The original Christmas story was not commercialized nor was it sold to the highest bidder. The original Christmas story was a baby born in a manger because there was no room in the hotel and, by the way, it was first shared with a group of outcasts: marginalized shepherds.

As the year 2020 comes to an end and our cities, nation, and world reflect on significant events, two very powerful events will leave indelible impressions.

- One, a global pandemic that took the lives of hundreds of thousands of people around the world.
- Two, people protesting in the name of Black Lives Matter as a result of historic racism and injustice.

After enduring a year when a pandemic and protests took place simultaneously, some may question the good news of Advent and wonder if there is still good news in the midst of sickness, crime, poverty, hunger and racism. The answer to the question is still the same today as it was in the time of Jesus: yes, there is good news.

There is Good News

What is the good news? The good news is that God truly has the whole world in God's hands and that there is healing, forgiveness and reconciliation for the land and God's people. As a Christian, I have hope in humanity, but most importantly I have hope in God and the work of Salvation of Jesus on the Cross of Calvary. I know that God's work through Jesus is complete and although I don't always see healing, forgiveness and reconciliation, I know it is happening and will be fully realized one day. The same way Jesus is for all people, healing, forgiveness, and reconciliation is also for all people. This is good news that is wonderful and joyous. In times like these we hear and receive so much bad news that is depressing and debilitating to the human soul and mind. If we aren't careful, we can open ourselves up to more bad news than good news and our challenge is to drown out the noise of the bad news and turn up the volume of the good news.

Ultimately, we call this good news "new life" and "salvation." It was shared by the angel. These shepherds were the first to receive the news of Jesus' birth, and now their lives were about to be transformed forever through the power of Jesus Christ.

The good news is that new life is possible at any point in time and that God's grace is available for all people:

> *Your savior is born today in David's city.*
>
> **Luke 2:11**

The angel told the shepherds they have a Savior and a claim to the inheritance of eternal life forever. The angel highlighted salvation through Jesus. Up until that time, sacrifices had to be made through priests on behalf of the people. To shed the blood of animals was the intermediary between God, the people and their sins. Jesus represented a personal Savior whose death and resurrection on the cross opened the way for grace, mercy and forgiveness for all people. These shepherds were beneficiaries of Jesus' life, and in one moment, they had an opportunity to experience new life in Jesus Christ. This was the greatest confirmation of salvation they could have ever received.

In John's gospel, salvation and shepherding are closely related and one example is Jesus saying:

> *I am the good shepherd. The good shepherd lays down his life for the sheep.*

John 10:11

It wasn't by coincidence that Jesus referred to himself as a "Good Shepherd," a role and position of lowly stature. Jesus was not only counter-cultural. He was also a radical as He shifted the norms and exchanged long standing traditions with the good news of love, acceptance and peace. This reflects how salvation is not always nice and neat. The work of salvation can be messy, radical and scandalous. Jesus Himself said that He loved everyone so much that He would lay down His life for them, and He held true to this promise on Good Friday. A Good Shepherd dying on Good Friday equates to our salvation. The road to Calvary and dying on the cross was not nice and neat, but messy, radical and scandalous.

The final phrase in verse 11 reveals continuity:

> *He is Christ the Lord.*

Luke ensures that the reader understands Jesus' life was not by luck or chance, but purposed in the mind of Almighty God. He is the one who, the prophets foretold, would save and redeem the world. This powerful word of continuity both confirms Jesus' birth to all the world and connects His birth to the announcement in Isaiah 9:6:

A child is born to us, a son is given to us, and authority will be on his shoulders. He will be named Wonderful Counselor, Mighty God, Eternal Father, Prince of Peace."

The Bible often builds on connecting one narrative to the next, and in the case of the New Testament Gospels announcing Jesus' birth, it is important for the reader to know that His birth is not an outlier, but it is connected to a point of origin which is the prophetic word in the Old Testament. The angel used a social media strategy to connect Old Testament prophecy in less than 140 characters and rocked the world of the shepherds with the breaking news of Jesus' birth. The continuation of prophecy is still being fulfilled today and God's promises are coming to pass.

I know there is much to fear and to be afraid of in the world today. There is sickness, loss of jobs, inability to make ends meet, frustrations at home, racism, ageism and sexism. These realities attempt to work against us each and every day and try to keep us from showing up and being our best selves.

Let me remind you to stay curious about the work of Christ in the world, but most importantly, know your own path, and know that God's best strategy to change the world is to begin with you. Similar to the shepherds, you may feel unnoticed, but God sees you and through Christ is offering new life. Don't turn away or become afraid. Let your faith make up the gap and exchange your physical sight for spiritual sight. When you use your spiritual sight, you will see that this new life isn't a new job, home or location but joy that is greater than the sadness in the world. Love that is more powerful than any hatred and faith that will give your biggest fear a run for its money. Maybe Advent this year isn't only about the masses, but also about you and what it means for you to hear the good news as if you are hearing it for the first time. Once you hear it, I hope you decide to surrender to Jesus and receive new life. As you light the rose or pink Shepherd's Candle, know that you are loved and that God sees you.

Questions for Reflection:

1. Have you ever seen an angel? If so, what did the angel look like? Did the angel say anything or was the angel present only?

2. Like Gideon, Zachariah and Mary, have you ever experienced an "With all due respect" moment with God, because what God was sharing with you was greater than your imagination could dream?

3. Have you ever settled for what you could see on the surface? What would it look like to explore more and trust that God will have your back?

4. What are you curious about in this season of your life and do you feel this may be one of those God moments?

5. In addition to Isaiah 9:6, are there other Old Testament scriptures that referred to Jesus birth? How have you seen those scriptures fulfilled?

CHAPTER FIVE
Emmanuel

Candle: Angel's Candle (Purple) / 4th Sunday of Advent

Symbol: Peace

Scripture: Matthew 1:23:

> ***Look! A virgin will become pregnant and give birth to a son, and they will call him, Emmanuel.***
>
> (Emmanuel means "God with us.")

Prayer:

> *Dear God, thank you for promising to never leave us and always remain with us. In times of confusion and chaos, give us peace and the reassurance of your love and presence. Thank you for every promise you have given us and every promise that has come to pass. In Jesus' name, Amen.*

Matthew's Gospel is chronologically first in the protestant New Testament, but scholars do not believe it was the first Gospel to be written. It is thought that Mark's Gospel was written first, and Matthew and Luke referenced Mark's gospel, as well as other sources, to build and develop their texts. One biblical historian wrote:

> *Sometime after 70 CE the Gospel of Mark arrived in*
> *the Matthean community, was accepted as part of the*
> *community's own sacred tradition and was used in*
> *its life and worship...The narrative of Mark became*
> *a fundamental part of the Matthean church's way of*
> *telling the Jesus-story....*[26]

Although Matthew's Gospel was not written first, it is highly referenced by lay and clergy citing or reading accounts of the Christmas story. Some of Matthew's highlights to the Christmas story are:

- Mary becoming pregnant by the Holy Spirit (1:18)
- Joseph having a dream and the angel telling him not to divorce Mary and to name the baby Jesus (1:20-23)
- Herod's attempt to kill Jesus and the family's escape to Egypt (2:13,14)

These stories have found their way into countless conversations, Bible studies, sermons and songs. In addition to an excellent script for a Christmas play, Matthew also gave us the benefit of tracing Jesus' lineage to Abraham and reminding us of the importance of continuity between the prophets and Jesus.

Matthew, like Luke, recorded Jesus' transfiguration on a mountain where His body was transformed, and "Moses and Elijah appeared to them, talking with Jesus"

---

26 Eugene Boring. *The New Interpreter's Bible. Vol VIII.* "The Gospel of Matthew" (Nashville: Abingdon Press, 1995), 95-96.

(Matthew 17:3). This linkage of people and stories is key and significant, and helps the reader transition from the prophets, patriarchs and matriarchs to Jesus and the Apostles.

From Beginning to the End

When I began reading the Bible, I typically read the Gospels and did not attempt much of the Old Testament. Whenever I read Matthew, I loved the way the gospel began with the birth and naming of Jesus as Emmanuel, which means "God with us," (Matthew 1:23) and ends with a powerful and often quoted declaration by Jesus, "Look, I myself will be with you every day until the end of this present age" (Matthew 28:20b).

It is important for Matthew to transition us from the prophets to Jesus seamlessly, and also for Matthew to remind us that God is at the beginning and the end. Therefore, whatever is in the interior, God can handle and see us through each and every situation. This bookend style approach to writing provides a sense of comfort and completion at the same time.

This is truly good news, especially as another year comes to a close. And, like you, I would never have thought this year would be one where people endured a global health pandemic alongside a global civil rights movement calling for an end to police brutality after the death of George Floyd and those who came before him who lost their lives at the hands of police officers. A pastor colleague, Dr. Tori Butler, on a Zoom webinar reflecting on the death of George Floyd and the subsequent protests, reminded the viewers

We have to lament our loss. [27]

Dr. Butler was right. During 2020, everyone has been touched by one form of loss or another and we are lamenting. 2020 has been a year of surprise, loss and lamenting:

- People are lamenting the loss of jobs, income and peace of mind.

- Others are lamenting the loss of loved ones and friends who passed from COVID-19.

- Some are lamenting the loss of the idea of justice and how social media videos posted of police brutality and vigilantly private citizens have dashed the hopes of those who held fast to the belief that freedom and justice was for all.

We were reminded of the historic "isms" that have crippled our democracy time and again, lamenting that the Beloved Community dreamed by Dr. King had not become a full reality.

In the midst of the COVID-19 pandemic and protests for justice in communities across the world, our worship team decided to dedicate two Sundays to answering singer/

---

27 "Lamenting. Listening. Leading: How the Church Can Respond.," Vimeo Video, posted by The Woodlands United Methodist Church, June 2020, https://vimeo.com/426292143.

songwriter Marvin Gaye's historic question from his 1971 hit song, "What's Going On?" The lyrics are a resounding plea to those in power and those who may choose to sit on the sideline of life instead of engaging in the fight for justice in their own unique way.

As you read these opening lines of the song, what do you feel, think and believe in light of where the world is today?

> *Mother, mother*
> *There's too many of you crying*
> *Brother, brother, brother*
> *There's far too many of you dying*
> *You know we've got to find a way*
> *To bring some lovin' here today.* [28]

The original score for the song was written by Obie Benson, a member of the Four Tops, after witnessing an incident of police brutality. Once he convinced Marvin to take the song, Marvin placed his magic touch by tweaking some of the lyrics, jazzing it up a bit, and the rest is history.[29]

The song was written and sung against the backdrop of a nation struggling with equality, war, poverty and injustice, and became a voice for people who were experiencing the struggles of life but could not seem to shape their experiences into words. Not only was "What's Going On?" a hit in 1971, the song also gave people the lyrics and music to a movement: a movement of protests for equality

---

28 Marvin Gaye. Lyrics to "What's Going On?" http://performingsongwriter.com/marvin-gaye-whats-going-on/. Accessed July 16, 2020.

29 Bill DeMain. (2006 June, Issue 94). Marvin Gaye's "What's Going On" Performing Songwriter. http://performingsongwriter.com/marvin-gaye-whats-going-on/.

and justice similar to the protests we've seen in 2020 with Black Lives Matter.

Writer Bill DeMain offered the following reflection of the hit song:

> *It was an immediate sensation, catching on radio in several major cities and selling over 100,000 copies in its first week.*

He concluded by reinforcing the song's legacy in history with the following words, "Beyond any chart position, the song has become a timeless spiritual anthem."[30]

Thanks be to God for anthems like "What's Going On?" that have always come at a time when people needed words, texts and language to protest their pain. Anthems have always found their way into society at just the right time, sometimes through the modality of speeches, marches, music and literature. I am not sure if these anthems are strategically coordinated or orchestrated, but they seem to come into being through a mixture of human determination and the spirit of change and justice.

Marvin Gaye's anthem was unique in that it not only made a statement, it raised a question. The question could not be avoided and caused listeners to contemplate and come to grips with the state of the world. Questions raised by anthems are good when they get to the heart of the matter and encourage dialogue, introspection and change. Fifty years after this hit song was released, we are still

---

30 Bill DeMain. (2006 June, Issue 94). Marvin Gaye's "What's Going On" Performing Songwriter. http://performingsongwriter.com/marvin-gaye-whats-going-on/

asking the question "What's Going On?"

- When will hatred end?
- When will equality be for all?
- When will all children, regardless of where they are born, have equal opportunity for success?

As you celebrate this Advent season against the backdrop of a health, economic and democracy crisis, and as you gather in person or virtually to sing Christmas hymns, you might be tempted to keep the oldies but goodies like "Silent Night," "The Little Drummer Boy" and "O Holy Night." Let me suggest you consider adding an additional song to your playlist this Advent: "What's Going On?"

Although this is a nontraditional Christmas song (and really not a Christmas song at all), it is a song that reflects the world in which we live and causes us to push away the pretty picture of a commercialized holiday and see a little town called Bethlehem in the midst of a broken world in need of a Savior. Like the '60s, '70s and 21st Century in America, our nation and world are still in need of a Savior, and the good news is that Emmanuel is here. Emmanuel can handle our concerns and questions.

Emmanuel brings the peace that Paul spoke of in Philippians, "And the peace of God, which transcends all understanding, will guard your hearts and your minds in Christ Jesus" (4:7 NIV).

I have often noted that it isn't that we don't understand peace intellectually, rather we don't understand how we

> **So often, we feel more comfortable asking Google questions than asking God.**

have peace in the midst of all that we go through. That is the power of Emmanuel, a peace in the midst of our storms and a constant source of comfort and strength. Unfortunately, many of us don't access the peace that Jesus provides and we find ourselves drifting and being tossed by anxiety and fear.

So often, we feel more comfortable asking Google questions than asking Jesus, but Jesus wants to hear your questions. Jesus is not overwhelmed by your fears and anxiety and is compassionate enough to hear our cry. Especially the cries of our children.

Who is our Neighbor?

A couple of years ago, our church staff received a startling update from United Way of Greater Atlanta about our community. The report was a "Child Well-Being Index,"[31] that showed how out of the hundreds of data points we hear about and see on the news, we could use just one score to predict the health of children and families in our communities. The information is important because "Of the nearly 1.3 million children living in our 13-county region, close to half a million live in communities with low or very low child well-being."[32] For East Point, Georgia

---

31 United Way of Metro Atlanta, Child Well-Being Index. https://www.unitedwayatlanta.org/child-well-being-overview/. Accessed July 16, 2020.

32 United Way of Metro Atlanta, Child Well-Being Index. https://www.unitedwayatlanta.org/child-well-being-map/. Accessed July 16, 2020.

where our church is located and much of our surrounding community, our Child Well-Being Score is 34.7 (red on the map). Think of it this way: children growing up in our community only have a 34 percent chance of reaching their full potential. This is simply not acceptable.

When a zip code is red, and has a score that low, it means there is a huge gap in the connections to children in that particular community, from schools, parks, health-care, food resources and jobs for parents. These basic support systems needed to thrive may not be adequate, accessible or bountiful as those in communities that are green on the map. Although math wasn't my strongest subject, I can see that things don't add up. You don't have to be a math genius to understand the scope of loss we risk if we sit back and allow the system to continue as is.

Our faith commitment tells us we have an obligation to look out for one another and right wrongs. The truth of the report was so evident and compelling that we began to take action as leaders in our church. The Child Well-Being Index guided conversations about how we could turn the curve on the score in our community. Change that red to green. Unleash the bountiful potential that exists in the more than 15,000 children growing up right outside our door. Specifically, we focused on seven key measures:

- % Low Weight Births
- % Students Achieving 3rd Grade Reading Proficiency
- % Students Achieving 8th Grade Math Proficiency
- High School Graduation Rate

- College & Career Readiness among High School Students
- % Children without Health Insurance
- % Children in Poverty

We had meetings and conversations with experts, and dedicated time during worship on Sundays to emphasize the state of children and families in our community. The conviction was so great, we tweaked our design for the next phase of development for our campus to help address the needs of our community. We called this next development step Phase 2A, and the goal was to renovate the remainder of the warehouse that we bought a few years earlier that I was anxious about. Now a few years later, my anxiety shifted from affordability to courage. As leaders of our church, would we have the courage to shift our design plans from what we thought we needed to develop to what children and families needed? My anxiety was lessened when we made the adjustments and had the hard conversations with key stakeholders. We are now moving forward with a design that is primarily about children and families. This adjustment decision wasn't easy, and I am sure we lost some people along the way, but it was the right call to make for the sake of being a 21st century Emmanuel Church. This decision was our answer to Marvin Gaye's question, "What's Going On?" We realized there could never be true peace in our community and world unless children were safe and they were being raised in environments that allowed them to reach their fullest potential.

So, what were some of the design and program adjustments? Initially, the largest part of the Phase 2A development was to add more seats for worship, but after reviewing the report and other data on our community, we pivoted and decided more seats for worship could wait until Phase 2B.

- We added an indoor gymnasium (student center) that will operate 24 hours a day and accommodate all indoor sports and activities.

- We added a commercial kitchen to help address food disparity in the community and plan to partner with chef entrepreneurs to help them reach their dreams of opening a restaurant or food truck.

- We doubled down on building thematic rooms for children and youth that would allow them to walk into spaces that resemble the professions they dreamed of one day pursuing.

- We will partner with professionals to mentor the students while they are in the thematic spaces.

- We have this outrageous dream of extreme after school programs where kids from local schools are bused to our campus, and upon arrival, the students are divided into groups A and B. Group A starts in the student center, where they have physical education training while Group B starts in the thematic spaces, where they complete their homework and receive academic enrichment support in English, math, science, literature, and foreign languages. Once the groups have spent the allotted time in each of the spaces, the students and volunteers will assemble for dinner in the large group meeting area. With the support of a commercial kitchen and healthy food partners and excellent volunteer chefs, the students and volunteers will have one of the best meals they have ever tasted that will include lively and inspirational conversations with their mentors. At the end of the day, the students will return home ready for a new day.

This plan is our way of changing the red zone for children and families in our community to a green zone. It answers the question, "What's Going On?" We decided as believers that it is not okay for one kid who is born in a green zone to have abundant opportunities for success and a kid born in a red zone to have less opportunities for success. We could not forget that Jesus' birth was about all people, and the wonderful and joyous news that the angels shared with the shepherds is still being shared today. In this instance, we hold dual roles. On one hand we are the angels sharing the wonderful and joyous good news with the world that there is hope.

On the other hand, we are the representation of Emmanuel on Earth and have to be witnesses through how we serve and show compassion to our brothers and sisters, especially our children. Being an Emmanuel Church and believer means we are part of the fulfillment of Jesus' Great Commission in our context. When we received the startling "Child Well-Being Index," I told our team we didn't have to pray anymore about what God wanted us to do and be as a church. The report was our answer to prayer, and now the responsibility was on us to be the hands and feet of Christ in our community.

As a believer, what do you do when God answers the prayer you have consistently prayed and shows you the answer? Do you receive the answer and keep praying or do you receive the answer and cease from praying and go and do the work?

Matthew begins by introducing Emmanuel in the form of a newborn baby in Bethlehem. Matthew ends with Jesus in His early 30s, being crucified, dying, being resurrected and commissioning His disciples. After instructing his disciples, He declared, "Look, I myself will be with you every day until the end of this present age" (Matthew 28:20b).

We know that Jesus wasn't saying that He would physically be with us, but through the presence of the Holy Spirit and the ministry of His disciples going into all the world, Jesus would always be with us. A critical part of His presence remaining with us on Earth is through the work of His disciples.

Historically, it is believed that Jesus had twelve disciples, but Luke's gospel refutes this belief:

> ***...the Lord commissioned seventy-two others and sent them on ahead in pairs to every city and place he was about to go.***
> **Luke 10:1**

Jesus had many disciples while He was on Earth, and now those many disciples have become billions of disciples today. The Pew Research Group estimated the Christian population "...remained the largest religious group in the world in 2015, making up nearly a third of Earth's 7.3 billion people."[33]

Wow! That's a lot of Christians.

More importantly, that is a ton of disciples of Jesus Christ. The way Matthew 28 will come to pass and the way Emmanuel (God with us) will be realized is by each of us as disciples of Christ seeing our place and role in the world. Our role isn't to complain, but to ask the deep and abiding questions that cause people to reflect and ultimately change their ways of thinking, behaving and believing. Our place as Christians is to help create the "Beloved Community" that Dr. Martin L. King, Jr. dreamed of, and when we have created this community, whether physical or virtual, the old saying will be true, "They will know we are Christians by our love."

The world Jesus was born into wasn't perfect, and if it was, there would have been no reason for Him to come to Earth. Jesus' mission was our salvation, and He left His disciples (you and me) to complete and fulfill the mission. To be Emmanuel to our friends, family and community will mean having to make some changes and adjustments, and even endure some struggles and disappointments along the way.

Our church made some big changes because it was

---

33 Conrad Hackett and David McClendon. "Christians Remain World's Largest Religious Group but they are declining in Europe." https://www.pewresearch.org/fact-tank/2017/04/05/christians-remain-worlds-largest-religious-group-but-they-are-declining-in-europe/. Accessed July 16, 2020.

more important for us to be Christ to our community and not just preach and sing about Christ. I believe the Holy Spirit is shifting and leading you in some ways that are unknown and uncomfortable for you and I pray that you will remain faithful and encouraged and go where God leads you. This is a season where courage is absolutely necessary, and the world is waiting on you to be the change you prayed to see.

This is a time for courageous leaders. Courageous ideas. Courageous risks. Courageous decisions. Courageous beginnings. Courageous endings. Being brave and courageous is always worth it.

The answer to Marvin Gaye's question, "What's Going On?" is *you*.

You are one of Jesus' disciples and part of the expression and reality of Emmanuel (God with us) on earth. This is peace for you personally and peace for the world. You can have peace in the midst of a global pandemic and historic injustices, not because everything is alright or you are out of touch with reality, but because you are tuned into and focused on the presence of God. When you recognize Emmanuel in your life you have a responsibility to tell others that God is with them and that they can have assurance and peace even in a world filled with chaos. The new challenge modern day disciples face is reaching people in the midst of social distancing, social distrust, and social injustices. Although on one hand some of what we are seeing is new, when we review history we note that each of these challenges always existed for Jesus' disciples and they found a way to fulfill the Great Commission. We are living in a season when it is the best time to represent Christ and be the Church, and it begins with you knowing who you are in Christ, and never forgetting that Christ will never leave you or forsake you.

You are the answer. You are Jesus' representative in the world. Go forth in authority and favor as you light the purple Angel Candle this Advent Season.

Questions for Reflection:

1. What does a 21st century Emmanuel believer and church look like? What are some examples?

2. Are there changes the Holy Spirit is asking you to make personally and professionally to answer the question, "What's Going On?"

3. Have you been praying and asking God to provide support and resources for those in need? Did God answer your prayer? If so, what was the answer?

4. Do you ever feel alone, and that God may not be with you? How do you manage through the moments when you feel alone?

5. What does brave, and courageous leadership look like in this season?

CHAPTER SIX
Claim and Reclaim Your Hope

Candle: Christ Candle (White) / Christmas Eve

Symbol: Light of Christ

Scripture: Luke 2:14

> ***Glory to God in heaven, and on earth peace among those whom he favors.***

Prayer:

> *Dear God, As we celebrate this Christmas Eve, we light the Candle of Christ as a reminder of Your grace and His sacrifice on the cross. As this candle is set aglow, His presence is a constant reassurance of love, peace and joy. Today we celebrate and remember the birth of Christ. Amen.*

The final candle to light during Advent is the Christ candle. In one article, the following description is given:

> *The Christ Candle represents the light that the Son brought into the world when he was born a little baby, God in the flesh. The fact that the Advent candles remain on Christmas Eve puts the focus on this special moment of birth, the moment of transition from prophecy to fulfillment." It goes on to say,*

"On Christmas Day and the Christmas Sundays, the Advent candles are usually removed, but the Christ Candle remains. This reminds us that old things have passed away, and all has been made new." [34]

As you experience Advent, remain open and expect the joy of the Lord to meet you at every point and juncture along the road of life. Expect there to be a transition from "prophecy to fulfillment."

This means that you are expecting God to fulfill the promises and prophecy in your life as well as the lives of those you love and care for. Some of these promises and prophecies may be:

- A new career
- Healing in a relationship
- The successful transfer of the family business to the next generation
- •Recovery from a long-term illness
- Getting or staying out of debt
- Building a legacy of joy, love and peace

It isn't easy waiting on the day of fulfillment because it can be a daunting and a lonely experience. You are having to depend solely on faith because the normal signs, symbols and road markers aren't there and even when you are careful, you can lose your way.

---

34 G. Goebel. *What is the Christ Candle?* Anglican Compass. https://anglicancompass.com/christ-candle/. (2017, December 24). Accessed July 16, 2020.

In these moments as you wait for the fulfillment of God's promise and prophecy over your life there has to be an invincible strength within that reminds you to keep moving and not to stop even when you are unsure of the direction you are traveling. It is the same strength we mentioned earlier that Joshua was commanded to have as he took over the helm as leader of Israel.

Although Joshua may have perceived he would be the next leader of Israel, he probably assumed Moses would at least hang around to coach him through a transition plan and then move off the scene, after being assured Joshua was ready to be the next leader.

In two powerful verses at the beginning of the Book of Joshua, the following is recorded:

> *After Moses the Lord's servant died,*
> *the Lord spoke to Joshua, Nun's son. He had*
> *been Moses' helper. "My servant Moses is dead.*
> *Now get ready to cross over the Jordan with this*
> *entire people to the land that I am going to give*
> *to the Israelites."*
> **Joshua 1:1-2**

In these two brief verses, Joshua had to shift from prophecy to fulfillment after having to say goodbye to his mentor.

For some of you, the shift from prophecy to fulfillment may be quick like Joshua's and your wait may not be as long, but you will still have to have faith through the process. For others, the shift from prophecy to fulfillment may not happen in your lifetime, and you will have to have the faith that helps you believe that it will be fulfilled in the next generation. In any case, God is telling you to get ready for a change, a shift and a new normal that you may not yet be fully ready for. Still, you have to move towards it anyway.

Strength is what we must have in this season as we are waiting and as God is fulfilling the promise and prophecy. You are stronger than you think and God has been preparing you for the time of fulfillment. I know it will be one of the greatest moments of your life.

The fulfillment of the promise and prophecy is not only for you, but for the world that awaits the coming Christ and their own fulfillment of God's promises and prophecies. Allow the light of Christ to guide you and to keep you and know that Christ will never leave you nor forsake you. The light and presence of Christ will be your Heaven on Earth, and although you may have lamented more than you would have liked to and found yourself crying more than praising, hold on in faith.

You are Part of a Lineage

Your faith will not disappoint you or fail you. You have the faith of your ancestors that carried them through times of uncertainty, and even when they knew their prayers would not be answered in their lifetime, they knew it would come to pass in your lifetime. Remember, you are the answered prayers of your ancestors. You are part of a lineage of matriarchs and patriarchs who were victorious and overcomers.

We listed some of those earlier in the book, such as Deborah, Mary, Zachariah and Gideon, but there are many other matriarchs and patriarchs we could list. Many of them you would have to announce because they are your parents, grandparents, great-grandparents and members of your family who had to overcome great trials to achieve their life's purposes. They were shining beacons of faith in your life and still inspire you today to continue pressing through in spite of the odds.

Like the Apostles in Acts 1, who with faith looked up during Jesus' Ascension, you can look forward because Heaven is before you and all around you. Every time you see a child smile, you are experiencing Heaven. When a co-worker sends you a text and tells you they appreciate you, that is Heaven. It is even Heaven when a relative reaches out because they know you are experiencing financial troubles.

The version of Heaven in the by and by – with mansions, streets of gold and reconnecting with family and friends who passed before you – will be a reality one day, but today, Heaven is also here and now. It is seeing the love of Jesus in the world and knowing your life matters and that life is always worth living.

God doesn't choose people or places based on external attributes or popularity. If this was God's desire, Jesus would have been born in pomp and circumstance and the whole world would have received the news of His birth before lowly shepherds received the news in the middle of

The version of Heaven with mansions and streets of gold will be a reality one day, but today, Heaven is here and now. the night. Jesus would not have built His ministry on the platform of saving the lost and defending the oppressed and marginalized.

When Jesus was selecting His disciples in John's gospel, and Philip told Nathanael about Jesus and His place of origin, Nathanael replied, "Can anything from Nazareth be good?" (John 1:46).

Too often we have measured and assessed people on the wrong metrics and thanks be to God, through Jesus, there is a new metric and assessment which is grace and love.

Even Jesus was discounted and discredited, and His humble beginning on Earth is hope for people living today. Especially those who feel discounted and discredited. Jesus was, is and always will be, the ultimate outsider who was born in a manger surrounded by animals, and who died outside on a cross and was placed in a borrowed tomb.

Your life and your legacy matters so much to God that God sent Jesus, not as a warrior king as people had hoped, but as a Savior to heal our world. The healing Jesus brought was forgiveness and grace.

Jesus is our wounded healer. By His wounds, pain, suffering, death and resurrection, we are healed. Not only are we healed through Jesus' wounds, but we are called to help heal others through our own wounds.

Henri Nouwen speaks of us as Christian leaders and as being:

> ...*people of hope whose strength, in the final analysis, is based neither on self-confidence derived from their own personalities, nor on specific expectations for the future, but on a promise given to each one of us. This promise not only made Abraham travel to unknown territory; it not only inspired Moses to lead his people out of slavery; it is also the guiding motive for any Christian who keeps pointing to new life even in the face of corruption and death.*[35]

We are truly a "people of hope" as we walk in the way of Christ living and being wounded healers. This hope is expressed in so many profound and wonderful ways. Perhaps the most important form of hope that we claim and reclaim as Christian leaders this season is forgiveness and grace. We have a moral responsibility to show and tell the world that there is more to Earth than what we see and experience. There is peace, hope and love. Most importantly, there is grace. Although we don't deserve grace, God loves us beyond our mistakes and failures. God's grace through Jesus is an all-encompassing love. This is what being an Emmanuel Church is all about and what it means to be Emmanuel for the world.

I have discovered that preaching to individuals has value, but the greatest value is embodying the sermons and songs that we love and demonstrating God's love and grace to the world. In our church's journey, this meant making some hard decisions around the development design for

---

35 Henri Nouwen. *The Wounded Healer* (New York: Image Doubleday, 1972), 81-82.

the next phase and for you it may be forgiving someone who hurt you, finding a new path after loss or accepting God's preferred call for your life after realizing you have been working in the wrong career for years. None of these decisions or paths will be easy, but when you dare to move forward you will be showing the world Jesus.

It is through forgiveness and grace that we receive new life. In Luke, when the shepherds (while in the middle of the field) received the announcement of the birth of Jesus, they were also receiving an opportunity for new life. An opportunity to trust in a Savior who had been prophesied about for hundreds of years, and they were the first to receive the news.

We are reminded that shepherds, who were not viewed highly by society, received the breaking news report first. The same way that God chose Bethlehem, God chose the shepherds, and God is choosing you today to receive new life. Receiving salvation is a part of new life, but it doesn't end with salvation. The goal is to live every day in the newness and revelation of Jesus Christ.

I love these words in Lamentations that reminds me of what life is all about,

> *Certainly the faithful love of the Lord hasn't ended; certainly, God's compassion isn't through! They are renewed every morning. Great is your faithfulness.*
>
> **Lamentations 3:22-23**

As you move through Advent and into Christmas and the New Year, expect God's love. Expect God's compassion.

Expect God's faithfulness. This is what life in Christ is all about. Being in Christ means that each and every day there is new joy, new peace and new hope. On any given day in your life, the negative things you hear and see can cause you to feel anxious, despair and sad. The reality of what you see and feel is real. It is true. All is not well in the world. But, Jesus is the alternative to the world and what we hear and see. Each day, we have to make a conscious choice and choose Jesus.

In this season, Jesus is waiting for us to surrender and know that there is great joy and peace in Him. That is why we light the Candle of Christ on Christmas Eve, because we light it in faith that the promise of Matthew 28 is true, and that Jesus never left us and never will leave us. Advent never ends.

As you take your Advent journey, I leave you with the words of the great theologian Howard Thurman from a meditation he wrote entitled, "The Christmas Candles."

> *Hope is the growing edge! I shall look well to that growing edge this Christmas. All around worlds are dying out, new worlds are being born; all around life is dying but life is being born. The fruit ripens on the trees, while the roots are silently at work in the darkness of the Earth against a time when there shall be new leaves, fresh blossoms, green fruit. Such is the growing edge! It is the one more thing to try when all else has failed, the upward reach of life. It is the incentive to carry on. Therefore, I will light the candle of hope this Christmas, that must burn all year long.*[36]

---

36 Howard Thurman. *The Inward Journey* (Richmond, Indiana: Friends United Press, 1961), 29.

I pray as you light your Advent candles the fire of hope and the presence of Jesus will never go out or go away. Reclaim and claim your hope and know as Thurman said, "Hope is the growing edge!"

Questions for Reflection:

1. What is the most significant of the Advent Candles to you? Explain your answer.

2. Where do you see traces of hope in the world today? How have you been able to encourage hope in your context?

3. How are you claiming and reclaiming hope this season?

4. What are tangible and current examples of grace in your life and the world?

5. How will this Advent Season be different from previous Advent Seasons? What will be different for you, your family, your congregation and your community?

CHAPTER SEVEN
The Year 2021

Since this Advent is different from those we've experienced in the past, I thought it would be appropriate to end this book differently. Typically, Advent books guide you through the end of the year. But considering the year we have experienced, I believe there is a need to go a little past December. Let's move on to January 2021 to ensure we don't get stuck after Christmas or become disappointed if we aren't able to sustain our New Year's resolutions.

Consider this closing chapter an Advent party favor. I hope that you keep this chapter as a reminder when the Christmas hymns are no longer playing in a loop on your favorite radio or satellite station, and when cable and streaming services aren't playing *It's a Wonderful Life, A Christmas Story, Home Alone* and *The Preacher's Wife* in a steady rotation.

It is a party favor to consider when the clock changes from 11:59 p.m. December 31, 2020 to 12:00 a.m. January 1, 2021, and you exclaim out loud, "I made it!" Yes, you would have made it through one of the most difficult years in modern day history. You reclaimed the promise you made to yourself that you would celebrate because life is precious and short. And the Psalmist was right, "The days of a human life are like grass: they bloom like a wildflower; but when the wind blows through it, it's gone; even the ground where it stood doesn't remember it" (Psalm 103: 15-16).

You are on top of the world, and your future is in front of you. You are ready for a New Year and a new perspective. You committed to looking, loving and learning. But in that very moment of celebration and commitment, something changes and shifts. Your countenance is no longer filled with joy and peace but concern and sadness. As quickly as you were celebrating and thanking God for a new year, the old you discovers your new address and knocks on your door. It is in that moment that you have to make a decision. You can choose to ignore the door and live your best life in 2021 in spite of the circumstances around you, or open the door and invite your past fears and doubts to have an old conversation with the new you. In that moment, remember this chapter, and look inside your party favor. Hold fast to these four phrases of hope: Don't Worry, Don't Fear, Stay Positive and Stay Curious.

Don't Worry

In Luke 12, Jesus is teaching His disciples about life, and He took the time to address worrying. Jesus said, "Therefore, I say to you, don't worry about your life, what you will eat, or about your body, what you will wear. There is more to life than food and more to the body than clothing. Consider the ravens: they neither plant nor harvest, they have no silo or barn, yet God feeds them. You are worth so much more than birds!" (22-24 CEB). At first glance, it would seem that Jesus is a little out of touch with the issues in the world and is inconsiderate of the responsibilities the disciples had outside of ministry. But after taking a second glance at the scripture and seeing Jesus' words on a deeper level, we see that Jesus truly understands the cares of the world and the responsibilities the disciples have.

The emphasis in Jesus' wisdom is on worth and value, and comparing their lives to the birds of the air. Jesus wanted them to know that although birds were important to God, their worth and value was even greater. If God has the capacity to care for birds flying in the air, then God has more than enough capacity to care for the needs of the disciples. In addition, if we are unable to change many of the things that happen in life, then worrying about them will not help us navigate life. Jesus' words of wisdom to His disciples is the same wisdom for His disciples living today and that is, "Don't worry."

I know you are probably thinking that is easier said than done. And you are correct: especially if you are a veteran at worrying and you didn't just start worrying in 2020.

As you transition to 2021, you may be tempted to recall that 2020 began as a great year, and as quickly as the year began your life abruptly changed without notice, and you spent the remainder of the year treading water and praying not to go under. As you begin 2021, something may happen or someone may say a word or phrase that reminds you about the sudden shift in the previous year and you will be persuaded to allow worry to fill your mind with a constant attack of doubt, anxiety and questions that can only be answered by God. This is when you have to hold on to your Advent confessions: Jesus is not on the way, Jesus is here. Jesus never left me; Jesus is always with me. Remain open and committed to looking beyond the surface to the extraordinary things God has in store for you.

I believe Jesus mentioned worry specifically because worry left unchecked has the power to drown out our possibilities and confine us to spaces that are too small and limited for our potential. We talked about daring to look below the surface for our potential, but there is also a reality of living above the surface in places that are too small or that we outgrew years ago. Worry is so powerful that when God increases our territory, vision and resources, we will still wonder if we deserved it or can sustain it. We have a tendency to forget our value, and consequently, stay in spaces and places that no longer feed or speak to our destiny. It is absolutely possible to walk into a new year with last year's worry and never fully capture the opportunities in front of us.

When you know how valuable you are to God, it is easier to step outside of the cycle of worrying and see God in everything around you. If and when you worry next year, place your concern next to Luke 12 and ask yourself the question, "Am I more important than what I am worrying about?" If the answer is yes, release it to God and know that God will help you manage the cares of this world. By the way, the answer should always be "Yes."

Matthew's gospel reassures us by beginning with "God with us" (Emmanuel) and ending with "I myself will be with you every day until the end of this present age." There is no care in this world that God can't provide or guide you through. Since God is at the beginning and the end, you are covered in the middle.

We are fully protected, and although the cares of the world are great, the God we serve is greater.

Don't Fear

Closely related to worry is fear. Towards the end of Luke 12, Jesus addresses fear, "Don't be afraid, little flock, because your Father delights in giving you the kingdom" (verse 32). Wherever there is worry, fear is close by, and it was necessary for Jesus to not only address their state of worry but also their fear. The disciples were along for the ride, and they had no idea what the future would hold.

Even when Jesus shared glimpses of their future, they didn't fully understand His words and could not grasp what He was teaching them. Although they didn't know, Jesus knew, and Jesus also knows our future as well, which is why Jesus encourages us not to be afraid. As it relates to 2021, I believe most people are afraid of the unknown and how easy it is for life to change at any given moment: to go from thriving and not being able to manage life in a single day.

To fear a New Year after experiencing 2020 is understandable because there are those who felt real fear for the first time this year and were unable to manage or control it. They realized there are some situations and difficulties that can't be avoided but have to be navigated. It would be ideal if we could sit down the last couple of months of the year and forecast the events of next year with assurance that everything will be ok.

Having this type of ability would give individuals, families, communities and corporations great relief. But this is wishful thinking. It doesn't exist because God is the only one who knows the contents of tomorrow.

In chapter 4, I mentioned that fear is contextual and that makes it more powerful. Like Gideon, Zachariah, Mary and Joseph, we have to come to a place where we can truly face our fears, and regardless of the outcome, dare to live our lives with faith and hope.

What if Gideon would have allowed fear to overwhelm him and keep him from being a leader in God's army and one of the judges of Israel? His leadership and legacy as a judge of Israel would have been missed and parts of the Old Testament text would have been adjusted.

What about Zachariah? He thought he and his wife Elizabeth were too old to receive the miracle of a child, and although he was afraid, eventually he saw God's hand at work and realized it was not about him but about what God was doing through him. His son John the Baptist is known throughout history because John's mother and father chose faith over fear.

We can never say enough about Mary and Joseph: how receiving word from an angel that they would raise the Savior of the world had to be one of the most fearful moments in their lives. Yet they found a way to keep looking and surrendered to be used by God.

Fear is dangerous because it can prevent us from surrendering to God's preferred plans for our lives. When we fail to surrender, God doesn't get the glory.

In spite of how hard 2020 has been for you, I believe that God has a plan for your life, and it is the plan that Jeremiah spoke of, "I know the plans I have in mind for you, declares the Lord; they are plans for peace, not disaster, to give you a future filled with hope" (Jeremiah 29:11).

Notice, the prophet is clear when he said, "I know." God truly knows how your life will begin and end, and if there is anyone you can fully trust with your life, it is God. The prophet also mentioned the word "hope" which we can't escape or deny. Hope is a word that I have held close to my heart. I believe hope is always possible, even in the most difficult circumstance. It breaks my heart when I meet people who have lost hope.

As much as I try to understand and get the full meaning of their despair, my mind can't help but wonder, "What happened and why did they lose hope?" James Weldon Johnson penned the beautiful words of "Lift Every Voice and Sing". In the third stanza, it speaks of hope in a way that I have contemplated over the years.

> *Stony the road we trod,*
> *Bitter the chastening rod,*
> *Felt in the days when hope unborn had died...*[37]

My thoughts on this verse and the use of the word "hope" take me back to a time in America when my slave ancestors were in bondage. Even though they believed and prayed, perhaps their hope died, and they were left in despair.

To think about this tragedy evokes feelings of sadness and mourning. Sadness because no one should ever feel or believe that hope is lost. Mourning because when one loses hope, it is as if they are losing life itself. The imagery of these lyrics is powerful and still applies to individuals living today who look out into the world without hope and wonder if they are valuable and have a purpose. It is true that one can suffer so much that hope may not survive, and this is painful to even consider and think about. In chapter 2, I mentioned the scripture from Romans 5:4-5 about hope, but there is another reference to hope towards the end of Romans, "May the God of hope fill you with all joy and peace in faith so that you overflow with hope by

---

37 Source: James Weldon Johnson, "Lift Every Voice and Sing." The Poetry Foundation. https://www. poetryfoundation.org/poems/46549/lift-every-voice-and-sing. Accessed August 8, 2020.

the power of the Holy Spirit" (Romans 15:13).

In 2021, don't lose your hope and don't allow your hope to die. What you fear and what you worry about is real, but even with great concerns about tomorrow, God will allow you to "overflow with hope" and through the journey of Advent, you will know that God is with you.

Stay Positive

I encourage you to stay positive next year and do your best to surround yourself with people and information that share good news and don't focus all of your attention on negative news. I am not telling you to deny facts and figures and not be informed, but I am saying don't limit your information flow to one platform or personality. You have to protect your mind and spirit, because what you allow to flow through them impacts your life and can literally change how you feel and believe on any given day or moment.

There was a time when I thought positive people were only born positive, and that there was some special gene in their DNA that preprogrammed them to always smile and share words of kindness with others. Now, after having the privilege of knowing many of these positive people, I understand it isn't a special gene that makes them positive but rather a choice. Some of these people have experienced horrific tragedies in their lives, and their survival is a miracle. Somehow as they walked through the pain and despair, God's grace and healing brought them to a place where they could see their whole life and come to a deeper understanding that each day, they had a choice to make. Although not easy, they chose life over death, faith over fear and peace over chaos. They didn't make this choice once, but each day they woke up they made the same consistent, positive choices. When people see them, they assume they are superhuman or have some unique skill set that allows them to overcome and persevere, but they don't.

They have the same option everyone else has, and that is a choice. The difference is that they choose to be positive even when they have the opportunity to be negative. These survivors are teaching us through their lives to choose joy as often as we can.

Next year, you will have a choice, and the choice is to be positive or negative. In our world, it is easier to be negative, pessimistic, cynical and critical, but the way of Christ is a different path and a better way. The way is the joy of the Lord.

Even as Jesus was dying on the cross, He was able to say, "Father, forgive them, for they don't know what they're doing" (Luke 23:34).

I don't think anyone would argue that Jesus would have won the #1 Positive Person award while He was living and while He was dying. I am sure that I could not have been as positive, hopeful and forgiving as people were cruci-fying me, if I were Jesus. Jesus teaches us to look forward, to do our best not to take the hurt and pain of yesterday into tomorrow and give tomorrow a chance for new life and new opportunities.

Advent compels us to reclaim that all is not lost and that hope is not dead. Hope and life are present right now. Maybe try saying to yourself, "Tomorrow will be better than today"; "Next year will have troubles, but I can face them and I will be okay"; "Even though I struggle with worry and fear, I am going to give life and living my best try and trust Jesus."

Stay Curious

Finally, we circle back and close with Brené Brown's thoughts on being curious about life and how curiosity uncovers the reality of uncertainty. But if we are willing to manage our uncertainty, the blessing and the fruit of curiosity is before us. I have always loved to see children explore, learn and play because they have a constant sense of curiosity.

They dare to ask questions adults believe are taboo. They have a resiliency that is unmatched. After they experience a fall on their bicycles, they may cry briefly, but after a smile and a hug, they are back on their bicycles having the time of their lives. Not only falling from their bicycles, but on their journey through childhood, they have a tendency to bounce back quickly from the scrapes, bruises and disappointments they experience.

The adults in their lives have to protect them from danger because they have absolutely no concern for the things that adults know may be harmful to them. They possess an everlasting curiosity that pushes the limits to the extreme. It is only as adults that these once curious children seem to lose their way. Unconsciously, they subscribe to the teachings of a mature society that says there are some heights that are too high, some distances that are too far, some exploits that are too dangerous and some forms of love that are too extreme.

At some point along the road of life, they may develop a new narrative and begin establishing guardrails around their curiosity that tells them this is too hot, too tall, too far, too much money, too many people and too much time. These narratives and phrases begin to be programmed into their minds such that when they meet a new person, opportunity, experience or New Year, before they can fully introduce themselves, their pre-programmed narratives take over, and the opportunity or chance is never fully developed. What could have been, never becomes, because curiosity dies at "Hello" or "Happy New Year!"

You can keep your curiosity alive by keeping Advent close to your heart and knowing that you are not alone in this life. Not only do you have people around you who love you, you also have Jesus, who will never leave you.

What is before you is tomorrow, and the next day and the day after and it is up to you to choose to live it with joy and peace or fear and anxiety. The joy and peace of Advent and the Christmas season will still be present in January. But you have to choose it and require it in your relationships and circles of influence because it is not enough for you to have joy and peace while others are in despair.

The light of Christ remains after the Advent season because the light is within you. Wherever you are, there is light and wherever you go, there is light.

Be the light.

Be the joy.

Be the hope.

Questions for Reflection:

1. Is there a fear in your life that you need to face? What is it?

2. Who could you call, text or go visit today to help relieve some of the fear in their life?

3. What is one step you could take to increase your positivity and reduce your negativity in 2021?

Lenten Studies

from Market Square Books

2021 Lenten Study
Journey to Transformation
Bishop Sharma Lewis

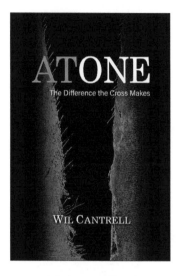

2021 Lenten Study
ATONE
Wil Cantrell

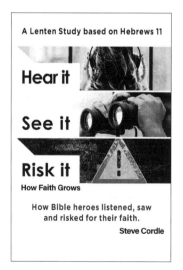

Hear It, See It, Risk It
Steve Cordle

Everything needed
for a small group
except the people!

NEXT GENERATION
SMALL GROUPS
Complete Kits for Virtual Groups

nextgensmallgroups.com

Recent Titles

from Market Square Books

marketsquarebooks.com

From Heaven
To Earth

Wil Cantrell & Paul Seay

Tidings of Comfort
and Joy

Charles W. Maynard

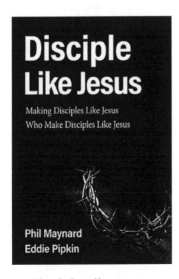

Disciple Like Jesus

Making Disciples Like Jesus Who Make Disciples Like Jesus

Phil Maynard & Eddie Pipkin

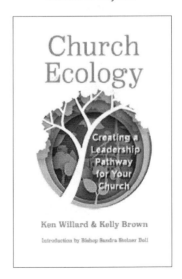

Church
Ecology

Ken Willard & Kelly Brown

Other Books
from Market Square

marketsquarebooks.com

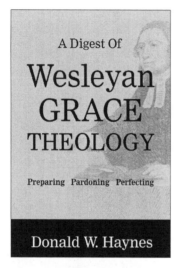

**Wesleyan Grace
Theology**

Dr. Donald Haynes

**Where Do We
Go From Here?**

24 United Methodist Writers

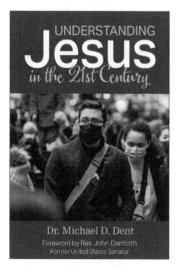

**Understanding Jesus
in the 21st Century**

Coming January 2021

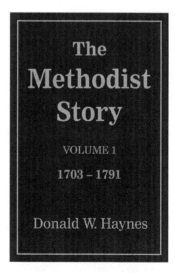

**The Methodist Story
Volume I ▪ 1703-1791**

Dr. Donald Haynes

Grow Your Faith

with these books from Market Square

marketsquarebooks.com

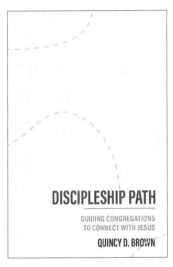

Discipleship Path
Guiding Congregations
Quincy D. Brown

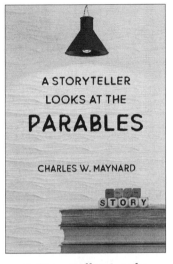

**A Storyteller Looks
at the Parables**
Charles W. Maynard

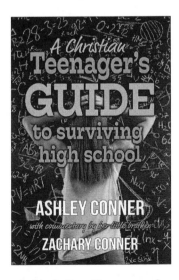

A Christian Teenager's
Guide to Surviving High School
Ashley Conner

Understanding Your Call
**11 Biblical Figures Understand
Their Calls from God**
by 10 United Methodist Leaders

Grow Your Church

with these books from Market Square

marketsquarebooks.com

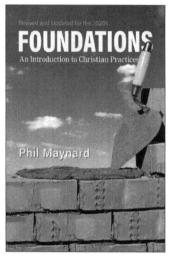

FOUNDATIONS

Phil Maynard

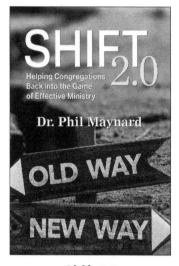

Shift 2.0

Phil Maynard

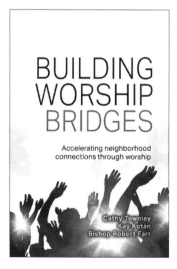

Building Worship Bridges

Cathy Townley

Get Out of That Box!

Anne Bosarge

Recent Titles

from Market Square Books

marketsquarebooks.com

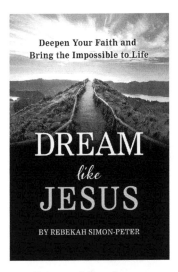

Dream Like Jesus
Bring the Impossible to Life
Rebekah Simon-Peter

From Franchise
To Local Dive
Jason Moore & Rosario Picardo

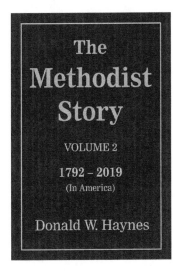

The Methodist Story
Volume 2 ▪ 1792-2019
Dr. Donald W. Haynes

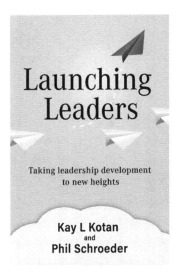

Launching Leaders
Leadership Development
Kay Kotan and Phil Schroeder